The BEAUTY of US

Also by Kristen Proby

The Fusion Series
Listen to Me
Close to You
Blush for Me
The Beauty of Us

The Boudreaux Series
Easy Love
Easy with You
Easy Charm
Easy Melody
Easy for Keeps
Easy Kisses
Easy Magic
Easy Nights

With Me in Seattle Series
Come Away with Me
Under the Mistletoe with Me
Fight with Me
Play with Me
Rock with Me
Safe with Me
Tied with Me
Breathe with Me
Forever with Me

Love Under the Big Sky Series
Loving Cara
Seducing Lauren
Falling for Jillian
Saving Grace

THE BEAUTY OF US

A Fusion Novel

Kristen Proby

wm

WILLIAM MORROW

An Imprint of HarperCollins*Publishers*

THE BEAUTY OF US. Copyright © 2017 by Kristen Proby. All rights reserved. Printed in the United States of America. No part of this book may be used or reproduced in any manner whatsoever without written permission except in the case of brief quotations embodied in critical articles and reviews. For information, address HarperCollins Publishers, 195 Broadway, New York, NY 10007.

HarperCollins books may be purchased for educational, business, or sales promotional use. For information, please email the Special Markets Department at SPsales@harpercollins.com.

FIRST EDITION

Designed by Diahann Sturge

Library of Congress Cataloging-in-Publication Data has been applied for.

ISBN 978-0-06-267487-6

17 18 19 20 21   LSC   10 9 8 7 6 5 4 3 2 1

The BEAUTY
of US

Chapter One

~Riley~

I'm done," I announce as I stomp into the bar and see two of my four business partners behind it. Kat, the bar manager and maybe the coolest woman I know, has her flaming red hair up in ringlets, and Mia, the master chef, has pulled off her chef hat and let her long black hair down around her shoulders.

They both look as exhausted as I feel.

"What, exactly, are you done with?" Mia asks as she pours herself a glass of red wine, batting Kat's hands out of the way. "I can do this myself."

"I have a system," Kat says, earning an eye roll from Mia, who passes the bottle to her, takes a sip from her glass, and walks around the bar to sit on a stool.

"Men," I say as I take the stool next to hers. The bar is pretty empty, as it's nearing closing time in the middle of the week. There's just the three of us and a man sitting at the far end of the bar, nursing what looks to be a Jack and Coke.

And I'm not even going to think about the fact that his profile is hot.

"You say that at least once a month," Mia says.

"I mean it," I reply, and nod when Kat offers me a glass of Mia's wine. "Fill the glass to the top."

"You're both killing me with your wine habits," Kat grumbles. "There's a correct way to pour a glass of wine."

"We're not fancy like you," I reply, and offer her a smile when she passes me my glass.

Kat simply shrugs and goes to work washing the few glasses in her sink. "So why has the male species pissed you off this time?"

"So, I went out last night with this guy," I begin, and take a sip of my wine, gathering my thoughts. "Let's say he was . . . *not my type*."

"In what ways?" Mia asks. "I mean, did he have blond hair instead of dark? Or didn't drive the right car?"

"You make me sound shallow," I say with a frown. "Those things aren't the deal breakers."

"We don't think you're shallow," Kat says. "What are the deal breakers with this one?"

"Well, he was super sweaty. Like, just-walked-out-of-the-gym sweaty. And at first I thought, well, maybe he's just nervous. I mean, we haven't gone out before, so that's pretty normal."

"Sure," Mia says with a nod.

"But, the longer we sit there, the more he sweats. And I'm

talking, he has to use his dinner napkin to keep wiping the sweat away the way Whitney Houston did when she was in concert."

"So, he's a sweater," Kat says, then grimaces. "Can you imagine how much he probably sweats during sex?"

"Ew." I wrinkle my nose, almost gagging at the thought. "No. No, I don't want to think about that. So, he's super sweaty and *smelly*. And it's really the smell that did us in."

The dude at the end of the bar chuckles and takes a sip of his drink. I ignore him and keep talking.

"So, aside from the sweating and the stench, was he nice?" Mia asks.

"I think so," I reply. "I feel like a horrible person, but I didn't hear much of what he said because I was too distracted by the rivers of sweat on his face, and the smell."

"Okay, that's pretty gross," Kat says with a nod. "I mean, in his defense, maybe it's a glandular thing, or anxiety, or he has large pores or something, but I don't think I could get past the smell either."

"Exactly," I reply, holding my glass up in salute. "And the guy last week didn't smell or sweat, but I guess he assumed that if he bought me dinner he could get in my pants. Which he can't."

The guy down the bar from us laughs again, and now I can't ignore him anymore. I turn to face him, and have to take a breath when I really get a good eyeful of him. He's tall, lean, and his forearms look fantastic in the rolled sleeves of his button-down shirt. His brown hair is a bit messy, probably from shoving his fingers through it.

And he's wearing black-rimmed glasses.

"Hi there," I say, getting his attention. He glances my way with seriously sexy green eyes and I have to remind myself that I am *done* with men. Because otherwise, I'd be tempted to ask him out.

"Hello," he says.

"Did you want in on this conversation?" I ask, swirling my wine.

"I don't think I have anything to add," he says with a shrug. "I'm just a guy."

"Maybe you can give me some insight into the brain of a man," I reply thoughtfully. "Because I'm stumped. Completely stumped."

"Well, I don't sweat like your last love interest," he says with a cocky grin, making me laugh.

"He was definitely not my love interest," I reply.

"And I'm no doctor, so I can't assume that he has a glandular issue like you suggest. Could have been nerves. I mean, you're a beautiful woman. It makes sense that he might be a bit nervous. Doesn't mean a man can't use some deodorant, though."

"Yes. Exactly. But what is it with guys thinking they can just jump right into sex? I mean, I'm not a hooker."

"Whoa," he says, holding his hands up and grinning. Damn him for having a killer smile. "No one called you a hooker."

"Well, I think it's sort of implied that they think of me that way when they take me out, buy dinner, and then get pissed when I don't put out. I'm way too picky for that. I have standards."

"As you should," he says in all seriousness. "Maybe you're just meeting assholes."

"Well, that seems to be all I meet," I reply, and sip my wine. "I mean, what do you have to say for the rest of your species? Because *lesbihonest*, this isn't worth a penis. None of this is."

He just tips his head back and laughs, long and loud, and it charms me. He throws back the last of fhis drink and turns in the stool to face me head-on. And then those incredible green eyes of his take me in from the tip of my Jimmy Choos to the top of my blond head.

"Maybe they're simply attracted to you."

"You don't get it," I reply with a sigh. "Attraction is fine. Flirting is fine. But since when has it been okay to not show any respect for the person you're with? I have so many doubts about the human race as a whole at this point. Sometimes I wish the *Enterprise* was real, and Chris Pine could sweep me away to the Death Star, and we could have a bunch of Jedi babies and stuff."

Mr. Man just stares at me for a moment, then scowls. "You've just combined *Star Wars* and *Star Trek*."

"Whatever," I say with a shrug. "It's all the same thing."

"No," he says, and clears his throat. "No, it's not the same thing at all."

"But you understand what I'm saying."

"No, I don't understand because you just *combined Star*

Trek and *Star Wars*. They're not the same thing, so everything you just said is . . . incomprehensible."

I roll my eyes and look to Kat and Mia for help, but they're just smiling and watching me banter with the stranger.

"You guys are no help."

"He's right," Kat says with a shrug. "And this is all fascinating."

"Not all men expect to have sex on a first date," he continues. "In fact, I would have to say that *most* men don't, unless they picked you up at a bar, and you were grinding on them on the dance floor all night, and you're twenty-two."

"None of those things happened," I reply.

"Well, then, I'd say he's just a jackass."

"There seems to be an explosion in the jackass population," I reply, and sigh, passing my glass to Kat for a refill.

"Where are you meeting them?" he asks, and I bite my lip.

"I don't want to tell you."

"Online," he says with a nod.

"I didn't say that!"

"Didn't have to. If you met him at the gym or the grocery store, or somewhere else in person, you wouldn't be embarrassed."

"I'm not embarrassed."

"Yes, you are. Otherwise, you wouldn't mind telling me."

"Fine." I sigh and rub my forehead with my fingertips. "I met them online."

"Stop that," he says.

"I don't know where else I'd meet people," I reply. "I'm at

work at least fifty hours a week. I don't do school or clubs or church, and I rarely go to the grocery store because I always eat here."

"I could stop feeding you," Mia interjects and I toss her a glare.

"I'm just saying, if you always do what you've always done, you'll always get what you've always gotten."

"I don't understand any of the words you just said." I squint at him, trying to process.

"Switch it up," he says with a grin. "Try to meet people somewhere else. I mean, you didn't meet me online, and I'm not an asshole."

"Sure, you're cute, and you *look* like you have your shit together, but I suspect that once I got to know you I'd learn that you have mommy issues and fourteen dogs."

"You might," he says with a thoughtful nod. "I do hide those things well. All I'm saying is, stop using the dating sites and try meeting people in real life."

"Yeah. Easy for you to say." I pout into my wineglass. "Do I need to send you some money for this counseling session?"

"Nah, the first one's on me," he says, tossing that crazy-hot smile at me again. "Just don't combine *Star Wars* and *Star Trek* anymore and that's payment enough for me."

He pulls a few bills out of his wallet and tosses them on the bar, then stands to leave.

"Have a good night, and good luck," he says.

"Thanks." Just as he's almost out of view, I call out, "Wait! I didn't ask your name."

"Trevor," he says, and my stomach immediately does at least four cartwheels. "Trevor Cooper."

"You're early," is all I can think to say. My cheeks are burning, my fingers immediately tremble. "You're not supposed to be here for two more days."

"I like to come early. Get the lay of the land, that sort of thing." He smiles and waves. "See you in a couple of days."

He walks away, and as soon as I hear the front door close, I turn to my friends and just stare at them in utter horror.

"Tell me that didn't just happen."

Kat snickers and Mia just flat-out laughs, slapping the bar.

"This is hilarious," Mia says with glee.

"No, it's not," I reply. "I look horrible, I sound like a fucking teenager who can't get a boyfriend. He's here on *business*."

I drag my fingers through my hair, then lean on the bar in despair.

"He wasn't here on business tonight," Mia says, and pats my back. "Besides, it's okay with me if he doesn't stay. I didn't want him here in the first place."

"No, it's not okay if he doesn't stay," I reply, and come up for air. "The fact that Best Bites TV wants to come here to film *Seduction* is a big deal, Mia."

"I know, you've told me."

"I mean, this will put us on the map globally. And I know you don't love the idea of a camera crew being in the kitchen, but it won't be forever."

"We've already had this conversation," she says with a frown.

"Not that it matters because I was just a complete ninny with the producer of the show *right here* in the bar."

"A *ninny*?" Kat asks with a grin. "I like that word."

"Yeah, well, it's not describing you right now," I reply with a sigh. "He must think I'm completely ridiculous."

"I don't think so," Mia replies. "He smiled at you, and looked you up and down like you're a heaping scoop of ice cream and he couldn't wait to eat you up."

"Whatever," I reply, and roll my eyes. "Now I have to pull it together and have a professional relationship with him. I'm the one that has to work with him, not you guys."

Since I'm the marketing and publicity expert in our five-some, working with Best Bites TV is all on my shoulders. Which is fine, and what I enjoy, but I've never failed so badly during the first meeting with a professional.

"I'm mortified. I have to quit and move to Mexico."

"Sun and drinks all day, Enrique on hand to service your every whim?" Kat nods thoughtfully. "Doesn't sound too bad, really."

"Maybe we should all go," Mia says with a nod.

"You'd hate it," I reply, and nudge her with my shoulder. "You'd worm your way back into the kitchen to take over the place."

"True. I'd better stay here."

"I don't think any of us needs to move away," Kat says as she stows away the last clean glass. "He didn't seem at all put off by your man crisis, Ri."

"Dear sweet baby Jesus," I mutter, and shake my head. "What is *wrong* with me?"

"You're letting these men get in your head," Mia says. "Seriously, stop trying so hard. My mom always says that love will happen when you're not looking for it."

"That didn't work either." I dig my fingertips into the muscles of my neck, making a mental note to call for an appointment for a massage. "I'm really not a desperate woman, you know. I don't need a man to complete me."

"You've never been desperate," Mia says. "It's not a bad thing to want someone special in your life."

"Exactly. That's a perfect way to phrase it." I grab my handbag and lean in to kiss each of them on the cheek before I walk away. "I'll see you guys tomorrow if I don't die of embarrassment tonight."

"Sleep well!" Kat calls out.

IT'S BEEN A long day. Hell, it's been a long year. I can't complain, though, because the restaurant isn't just thriving, it's bursting at the seams. At the rate we're going, I can see us expanding to other Pacific Northwest cities in the next three years. We're always packed, and now that the television show is going to happen, we'll be turning people away.

It's something to be proud of, and maybe a little scared of too. When Addie, Cami, Mia, Kat, and I opened less than two years ago, we didn't anticipate this at all.

We just wanted the restaurant to be successful, to support ourselves, and we did that and more in the first six months.

But success is also exhausting, and that's exactly where I am tonight. Exhausted. Why am I using so much energy on meeting men online when I should be focused on work?

I'm happy and independent. But damn it, I see Addie, Cami, and Kat with their men and I can't help but be a tiny bit envious at the bliss they've found. The guys don't pull them away from the business; they support it too, and help in any way they can.

It's a team effort.

I want to be a part of a team.

And, I really do want to get laid on a regular basis. I mean, I'm a red-blooded woman, and I have needs.

And standards.

The drive to my house in Hillsboro doesn't take long, and soon I've changed into blue yoga pants and a coral tank top, sitting in my favorite chair in the corner of my bedroom, my laptop in my lap.

I feel like I should send Trevor an e-mail and apologize for tonight. What he heard is the epitome of unprofessional, and that's not the way I want our professional relationship to begin.

But I don't need to dig the hole any deeper. Sometimes it's best to just keep your big mouth shut. I have a master's degree in marketing and publicity, and that would be my first piece of advice to any client in this situation.

Less is more. Stop talking.

I nod, deciding to take my own advice, and open the laptop. I work my way through four of the online dating sites that I've subscribed to. I have messages waiting in each of them, from men I've never seen before, and a few that I did go on a date with, and it was definitely not a match.

Including Sweaty Man.

Hi Riley,

I had a great time last night. Let's do it again soon!
                                                    Greg

No thanks. I type out my typical *"it's not you, it's me"* response and hit send, and then I shock the shit out of myself as I methodically unsubscribe from each site, erasing my profiles.

This isn't working.

Maybe Trevor was right. Just stop it. Meet someone organically.

Or just die an old maid. I'm sure there are worse ways to go. Like, I could have a fatal skin disease or something.

Dying alone doesn't seem quite as bad in comparison.

I'm just about to close the computer and head to bed when there's a notification that I have new e-mail.

I'm about to ignore it for tonight, but the name "Trevor Cooper" shows up in the sender's name, and I can't open it fast enough.

Riley,

I'm writing via my personal email, as this doesn't pertain to our professional relationship. I wanted to apologize for this evening. I should have introduced myself when you first came into the bar. I wasn't expecting the conversation that began upon your arrival.

*Please accept my apology. I look forward to seeing you
in a few days.*

> *Warmly,*
> *Trevor*

P.S. The Death Star is in Star Wars. *It's also been
destroyed, so you can't go there. Sorry.*

I grin and read through the note twice more. Okay, this
was a nice guy move. Trevor is obviously kind, and maybe a
bit of a *Star Wars* geek.

But he's temporary, and a colleague. So the attraction I
feel for him doesn't count.

At all.

It doesn't matter that he's cute and smart and has a
great job.

Doesn't matter at all.

And I just gave up on dating as a whole, so there's that.

Chapter Two

~Trevor~

I didn't sleep worth shit last night. I waited for a response to my e-mail from Riley for a while; I'm not exactly sure why. I just don't like the thought of her being embarrassed.

Because she has no reason to be. She didn't know who I was, and it was closing time. She was venting to her friends.

It's really no big deal.

But I could see the mortification in her big blue eyes when she realized who I was, and that doesn't sit well with me.

When no response came, and for all I know she hasn't even read the e-mail yet, I sat down for a game on the PS4. I don't travel anywhere without it. Some people read to unwind. Some go to the gym, and there are times I do the same. But to truly relax, I enjoy gaming. I have since I was a kid.

So I settled in the apartment the network has rented for

me this month and played online with my friends, talking about our days and shooting the enemy.

We played well past midnight, and I usually would have gone right to bed afterward, but my mind was still turning, making falling asleep impossible. The restaurant is better than I imagined through my research on their website and customer reviews. It's visually stunning, the food is fantastic, and they've hit the mark on the sexy factor.

But added to that, the five women who own the place are all beautiful, smart, and will make for great TV. Viewers will eat this show up, pun intended.

I lean over the sink and wash my face, not bothering to shave today, and as I dry off, I reach for my phone.

I have several new e-mails.

The most recent is from Riley Gibson.

Trevor,

> *Thank you for your kind email. I apologize again for the conversation last night. I would like to promise that we don't always talk like that at work, but that would be a lie. At least we keep it to closing time over a glass of wine.*

Enjoy Portland,
Riley

I grin and sling the towel over my bare shoulders. Riley isn't what I had pictured in my head before I got here. I knew that she was pretty because their photos are on their website, but she's much prettier in person.

And animated.

Working with her will be fun.

And a test to my libido. Because Riley is fucking sexy. I've never mixed business and sex before, and I don't plan to start now, but keeping my hands off her will be a test of wills.

And that too should be fun.

After my run this morning, I stopped by a bagel place to eat and read a newspaper, came back to the apartment for a shower, and I think I'll go to Seduction for lunch. I hadn't planned to go back there until my meeting with Riley tomorrow, but I also haven't had lunch there yet.

I dress quickly in jeans and a red T-shirt and walk the six or so blocks to the restaurant.

They've just opened, so they're not busy yet. The atmosphere is calm, the lighting a bit brighter than last night, making it a fun spot to meet with colleagues or friends for lunch.

I'm seated on the far side of the restaurant, where it meets the bar, and I can see Riley and the other women sitting around a high table, talking.

Loud enough for me to hear.

"So, he'll be here tomorrow. Filming doesn't start for another week, unless the timetable has been moved up," Riley says, studying her iPad and checking things off a list. "It would be great if we could watch our language."

"Right," Mia says, rolling her eyes. "Because that's gonna happen."

"Just watch the F-bombs then," Riley says with a grin. "And I'll do my best not to vent to him about my horrible dating experiences. Not that I'll be having any more of those."

"I wish I'd been here for that," Addie says with a smile. "It's hilarious."

"No, it's not," Riley says, but smiles and covers her lips with her fingers. "Okay, it's a little funny. I'll be working from home today."

"Why?" The blonde speaking, I presume Cami, asks.

"Because I have a roofer coming today," Riley says. "But if you need me, just call. I can come back after he leaves."

"Go." Mia waves her off. "We've got this."

The girls all stand, about to go their own ways to get their day started. They're clearly good friends, which will come across well on film.

Riley walks out of the bar and glances up, spotting me.

"Hi." I offer her a smile and motion for her to join me. She sits, sets her iPad aside, and squares her shoulders.

I love a woman with grit.

"Why are you here?" she asks.

"I'm having lunch," I reply, and gesture to the salad sitting in front of me. "It's delicious. Adding the brussels sprouts is smart."

"I'll pass that along to Mia," she says, and then laughs. "I guess you heard the part where I asked the girls to not swear."

"I did," I reply, and patiently butter a piece of warm bread. "Don't worry about that stuff. They're adults."

"With potty mouths," she says.

"And we can bleep stuff out, or ask them to rephrase. You've already got the gig, Riley. I wouldn't be here otherwise. This isn't an audition."

"I know." She sighs and reaches over to take a piece of my bread, surprising and delighting me. "I just want things to go smoothly."

"Perhaps you should order lunch too."

"I don't have time," she says, and then her blue eyes widen as she realizes what she just did. "I'm so sorry. I eat when I'm stressed out, and I didn't—"

"No." I hold my hand up to stop her. "It's fine. I like that you're relaxed with me. I think you need to relax more often."

"What are you, my life coach now?"

"If you like. Did you cancel those dating sites like I suggested?"

She bites her lip and looks to the side, then nods. "I did."

"Good." I take a bite of salad and nod. "Are you sure you don't want some food?"

"I rarely have time to eat," Riley says, and checks the time on her phone. "In fact, I should go. I have to meet the roofer at my house."

"What's wrong with your roof?"

"It's old," she says with a shrug. "That's what happens when you buy an old house. I'm fixing it up a little at a time."

I nod, and find that I don't want her to go quite yet. I want to talk more, to learn more about her.

"Why don't you come to my apartment tonight and I'll cook you dinner?"

She pauses and stares at me for a moment. "Why?"

I laugh and set my fork down. "Because I asked you to. We're going to be working closely over the next few weeks, we might as well get to know each other a little better. Also, we can discuss my new duties as your life coach."

"Well." Her lips twitch as she thinks it over for a moment, a myriad of emotions moving across her beautiful face, and finally she says, "Okay. Do you mind texting me the address and the time?"

"Not at all," I reply, and immediately pass her my phone. "Plug in your number and I'll text you this afternoon."

She complies, passes it back, and smiles. "Okay, see you later."

And with that, she's off. Her ass swaying enticingly in her tight skirt, calves flexing from the height of her heels, and the food I'm currently chewing immediately tastes like cardboard.

Jesus.

And I just voluntarily offered to spend time with her. Alone.

I'm a fucking glutton for punishment.

"I'M STARVING," RILEY immediately says as I open the door. She's in jeans and a well-loved University of Oregon sweatshirt, her hair is pulled up in a ponytail, and she looks like she could be a co-ed herself. "I forgot to eat today."

"Does that happen every day?" I ask as I gesture for her to come inside and close the door behind her.

"Most days," she admits. "Is this one of those bad choices that you're gonna coach me through?"

"Yes," I reply, and lead her into the kitchen. "You have to eat."

"I know, I just get focused on other things, and the next thing I know, the day is gone and I'm starving." She passes me two bottles of wine. "I didn't know what we were having, so I brought red and white."

"Thanks." I grin and set them both on the counter. "I made salmon and asparagus with baby red potatoes. What goes best with that?"

Her eyes light up. "The white. Holy shit, are you a chef yourself?"

"I went to culinary school," I reply, and squeeze some lemon on the salmon before plating it. "But I discovered I was better at a desk job."

"That's unusual," she says, her head tilted to the side as she listens. "Most people fight to get out of a desk job."

"Not me. I have a ton of respect for Mia, because being a chef isn't easy, and pleasing people sucks."

"True." Riley nods. "She doesn't get many plates sent back to her, but there are a few. Can I pour you a glass?"

"No thanks," I reply, and reach in the fridge for a bottle of water. "I don't drink alcohol."

"Oh." She frowns. "I'm sorry. I can drink water too."

"It's fine," I reply, and pat her shoulder. "I don't mind if you drink. I just don't."

"But last night, you were drinking Jack and Coke."

"Nope, just Coke."

She sits at the table, still frowning. "I'm sorry."

"There's nothing to be sorry for." I set our plates down.

"I've been sober for ten years. I'm not the kind of alcoholic who can't be around others having a drink. It was never that bad for me. I'm just a better person if I don't drink."

"Good for you for knowing that," she says, holding her glass out to clink against my water. "This looks delicious."

"You sound surprised."

"I expected pizza or Chinese takeout," she says. "Honestly, that's probably what you would have gotten from me. I'm also surprised that you're not staying in a hotel."

"I'm here long enough that the network sprung for the apartment. They usually do when I'm somewhere longer than a week or so."

"You must travel a lot for this job," she says, eating her food like a starving child. I don't know if she even tastes it, she's eating so fast.

"I travel often," I reply, and grin when she takes the last bite. "Are you going to lick the plate?"

"Maybe," she says with a grin. "I'm not even embarrassed that I ate that so fast. It was delicious."

"I'm glad you liked it. There's more."

"No, I'm good," she says, and reaches in her bag, pulling out a pad of paper and a pen. "You can eat while I interview you."

"For what?"

"For the position of life coach," she says with a sassy grin. I want to kiss that grin right off her face, but instead I take a bite of potato and gesture for her to begin.

"Okay, first question: What qualifications do you have that make you a good fit for this position?"

"Well, I have a few years on you, so I would say wisdom with age."

She tilts her head to the side, the way she does when she's turning something over in her head. "You can't be that much older than me."

"I'm thirty-seven."

"Seven years," she says, rolling her eyes.

"A lot can happen in seven years," I reply, and sip my water.

"Okay, I'll give you that." She checks something off on her paper.

"Did you really write down questions?"

"Of course. I'm the queen of lists and the roofer was at my house *forever*." She bites her lip as she looks at her list. "How many women have you life-coached in the past?"

"Well, I didn't have an official job title, but I have two younger sisters, and an ex-wife, so I would say three."

"But the wife is an *ex*, so maybe that didn't go well?" Riley asks. "And are your sisters productive members of society?"

"As opposed to being in jail?" I ask, laughing. "You're hilarious, Riley."

"You didn't answer the question."

"My sisters are great. The older one is married, a stay-at-home mom with two kids, and the younger one is a waitress."

"But the ex-wife thing didn't work out."

"She's not a mess, we just both decided that she shouldn't be my wife anymore."

"Why?"

I sit back in my chair and wipe my mouth on my napkin. "Because she thought it was a good idea to have sex with other men."

Her eyebrows climb on her forehead and she blinks twice. "That's a good reason."

"I thought so."

"Okay, next question." She checks something on her paper and looks up at me with a smile. "How do you intend to be compensated for your work?"

"I'm working pro bono," I reply with a wink.

"Why?"

"Because I'm going to be here anyway, and why not." I shrug and finish the food on my plate. "What else do you want to know?"

"Is my coming to a virtual stranger's apartment by myself one of the bad decisions you should have coached me on?"

I smile and set my plate aside so I can lean on the table. "Did the girls tell you that coming here by yourself was a bad idea?"

"I only talked to Cami and she thought I should come. Plus, I have a concealed carry, so I feel pretty confident that I'm safe."

I raise a brow and cross my arms over my chest. "You carry a gun with you?"

"Hell to the yes," she replies, and offers me a sweet smile. "I've been meeting strange men on the Internet. You bet your ass I've been armed."

"Good idea," I reply with a nod. "There are a lot of crazies out there."

"Yes. But I think that if you're gonna meet a crazy, it could be anywhere. Online, in a bar, at the gas station. They're everywhere."

"That's true too," I reply, and nod. "Well, I'm glad you're being cautious."

"I'm nobody's victim," she says, as casually as if she's telling me her shoe size.

That's fucking sexy.

"Do you have any other questions?"

"Not really," she says, and shrugs. "I didn't really write anything down. But it was fun to interrogate you a bit."

"Now *I* have questions," I reply, and smile when she cocks her head and purses her lips. "Do you really think you need a life coach?"

"No, I have my shit together," she says with a grin.

"Why were you really on all of those sites?"

She shrugs. "Because it's not easy meeting people. And sometimes a girl wants to go out on a date."

"You don't need me," I reply, and smile. "But I'll be around for a while, just in case."

"Just in case I slip and fall back into the online dating?"

"That, or if you just want to have dinner, or chat. And I think we should watch a marathon of *Star Wars*. Your lack of knowledge is cause for concern."

"It's kind of a guy thing," she says.

"I know many women who like *Star Wars*."

"Well, I would watch one or two."

"You need to see them all to understand what's happening."

"That's a lot of hours of my life that I'll never get back," she says with a frown. "Aren't there CliffsNotes somewhere? A speedy way to get caught up?"

"No," I reply, and fist my hands in my lap so I don't reach out and tuck her hair behind her ear.

Or yank her against me so I can kiss the fuck out of her.

"Are you okay?" she asks.

"Are you always this observant?"

"I'm an overthinker," she says. "So yeah, I'm an observer."

"I've been labeled an overthinker too," I say with a grin.

"Would you say it's an accurate assessment?"

"Oh yeah," I say with a nod, and stand to clear our plates away. She stands to help. "I've got this."

"No way, you cooked, so I'll help clean."

She walks ahead of me, her empty glass in one hand and her plate in the other. "Do you use the dishwasher, or do you wash by hand?"

"There are people who still wash by hand?"

"I've heard of them, but I've never seen them in the wild," she says, and smiles up at me when I join her. "So I guess that means we use the dishwasher?"

"Yes." She rinses and I load, and a few short minutes later, we're done.

"Well, I suppose I should go," she says, and checks the time on her phone. "Oh, Cami texted. I guess I should reply so she doesn't think you killed me after the entrée."

She smirks and types on her phone, then turns it off and looks up at me.

"Thanks for dinner."

"You're welcome."

"I'll see you tomorrow morning."

Unfortunately, it won't be in my bed.

"You will."

"Okay." She gathers her bag, notepad and pen, and walks to the door. "Sleep well tonight."

I grin and congratulate myself for not dragging my fingertips down her cheek.

"*You* sleep well tonight, Riley."

"Okay. Bye."

She leaves and I close the door, letting out a slow breath. Jesus, she's sexy and funny and smart as fuck.

And I'm not going to touch her while I'm here.

How the fuck am I going to do that?

Chapter Three

~Riley~

*H*e's wearing a suit today.

A motherfucking suit.

Trevor walked into Seduction at seven this morning, carrying Starbucks for all five of us, an orange-and-white backpack slung over one shoulder, and his tall, lean body in a dark gray suit with a red tie.

It's been a week since I had dinner at his place. I've seen him at work, prepping to begin filming, which starts today, and I've spent time with him away from work too.

But he's never worn a suit.

"You're staring," Addie whispers in my ear as she joins me at the table of the empty restaurant. We're doing interviews early in the day, before we open for lunch.

"No, I'm not," I reply with a frown.

"It's okay," she says, and nudges my shoulder with hers. "He's pretty hot."

"I didn't think married women were supposed to notice things like that."

She smirks. "I'm married, honey, not dead. Trevor is a sweet guy, and the package is delicious."

"I've never seen him in a suit before," I mutter. "It's hot, right?"

"Hot," Addie confirms. "And his glasses?"

"Don't get me started." I shake my head and squirm in my seat.

"You've been spending a bit of time with him."

I frown again. "We're just friends."

"Oh, I know."

My gaze whips to hers. "Why do you say it like that?"

"Like what?"

"Like you're terminally disappointed in me."

"I didn't mean it like that. But Trevor is sweet, with a good job, and he's sexy. You seem to attract the exact opposite of that."

"Like you used to, before you met Jake," I remind her, and she nods with a grin.

"Exactly."

I look back to where Trevor is chatting with a camera guy. He nudges his black-rimmed glasses up his nose and shakes his head, adamantly against whatever the other man just said.

A muscle in his jaw ticks, and I have to look away.

"I can't be into him," I whisper to Addie, who just scowls.

"Why ever not?"

"Because he's only here for a couple of weeks," I hiss.

"You're not marrying him, Ri, but you might have a bit of fun."

"Do *not* say the sexcation word," I reply. "Kat already won in that game."

"And how," Addie says with a laugh. "Who knew that a sexcation could turn into love? Anyway, you're not on vacation. But it's okay to enjoy him. You guys seem to like each other."

"He's easy to talk to," I admit. "I don't get sick of him after three minutes. At least, not yet."

"If I was you," Addie says quickly just as Trevor glances our way and begins to walk over, "I'd enjoy the fuck out of him."

"Ladies," Trevor says with a smile as he approaches. Oh yeah, I'm attracted to him. I mean, the man is tall, and although I haven't seen him without clothes, I can tell that he takes care of his body.

And the way he smiles when I've said something to make him laugh? Holy baby Jesus, it makes me tingle.

"Who's first?" he asks.

"Sorry?" I have to clear my throat and pull my thoughts away from sexy Trevor and focus on work Trevor.

"Who are we interviewing first?" he asks again.

"Kat," I reply, and look around for her. "She has an interview for a new bartender soon, so she's going first."

"Great," he says, and winks at me as he turns to look for Kat.

"He likes you," Addie says.

"Oh, goodie. Be sure to tell him in study hall that I like him too." I roll my eyes and open my folder for today's itinerary.

"Whatever," Addie says with a laugh. "I'm just glad that you guys get along so well, since you have to work together. He seems nice, and if you're just friends, that's cool too."

"Just friends," I stress, and make a note for Cami's interview later this morning. "I hope the interviews don't go too long. We're running a bit behind."

"We'll only get three in this morning," Trevor says, surprising me. I glance up to see him standing at the table, arms crossed over his chest. "We'll do the other two tomorrow."

"Okay," I reply with a nod as Addie stands and walks into our office. "That makes sense. That way, if we go over we have wiggle room."

"Are you all chatty?" Trevor asks.

"We can be, especially when we talk about Seduction because we love it so much."

"That's awesome. Should make for some good footage, then." He points to the stage, where we've set up a table and chair for each of us to sit in for the interview. The camera and lights are set up and ready to go.

Kat is seated at the table, looking awesome in her blue rockabilly dress, her lips red and hair up in a fun ponytail.

"Are you doing the questions?" I ask him.

"Yep. You're welcome to watch."

"Oh, I planned on it," I reply. I'm nervous about this. I

mean, I trust my friends. They'd never say or do anything to jeopardize our business, but they're also very outspoken.

Especially Kat.

I stand, gather my notes, and walk with Trevor to the stage. We're both sitting out of the range of the camera. Kat looks beautiful under the lights; very sophisticated, fun, and put together.

Which describes her to a T.

"Are we ready?" Trevor asks the sound and camera people, who both nod.

"The sound guy and I should be going out to dinner later," Kat says with a wink. "He's been up and down my shirt all morning."

"Well, now we can hear you," Trevor replies with a grin. "And I'm quite sure the up-and-down-your-shirt thing was as horrible for Shawn as it was for you."

"Horrifying," Shawn says with sarcasm as he holds the sound equipment, big earphones on his head, and a boom overhead.

"Let's get started," Trevor says as yet another production guy holds the clapboard in front of Kat.

"Interview with Kat, take one."

"This is all very official," Kat says with a grin.

"Kat, can you tell us a bit about yourself, where you come from, and how you came to be friends with your four business partners?"

"Sure," she says, and shifts her gaze to mine. I don't think I've ever seen Kat look nervous, until today. I smile with reassurance and give her a thumbs-up. "I was raised here in Portland and also in California. My parents are scientists, and work in both places.

"I was homeschooled, graduated from high school early, and went to college at sixteen, which is where I met Mia, Riley, Addie, and Cami."

"And how did the five of you end up opening a restaurant together?"

"I think it was Riley's idea," she says, looking to me for clarification. "It just made sense, because with all of our individual talents, we each bring something special to the restaurant."

"And how did you come up with the theme of the restaurant?" Trevor asks.

"That was Riley's idea too," she says with a grin. "And I think we were all over at Addie's place, drinking too much, thinking about how we wanted to go about the business. One thing that we all decided on was that while there are plenty of delicious places to eat in Portland, there really wasn't one that catered to couples. I mean, if you want to go on a date with someone you're in love with, or even just interested in, you want to go somewhere fun and romantic. We really wanted the restaurant to be an extension of the romance experience. So Mia researched the hell out of aphrodisiacs and how to incorporate them into a menu, and the rest is history."

"It's such a smart business move," Trevor says, and I feel myself sit up straighter, proud of what we've done here.

"We've had probably close to two dozen marriage proposals here, and I can say with confidence that we're a great place to bring a first date," Kat says with a nod. "We truly wanted all of the senses to be titillated at Seduction."

"Can you tell us about the bar?"

"My baby," Kat says with a sassy wink, and I can feel myself start to relax, just a bit. She's doing so great!

"Well," she continues, "if you want to have a restaurant that caters to adults, it makes sense to have a bar in-house. I've always been interested in wines, how to pair them, how to serve them, and so on. We have an extensive wine cellar, but if wine isn't your thing, we have hard liquor and local beers as well. But I have to say, if you don't like wine, we can't be friends."

We all laugh as Kat flips her ponytail over her shoulder.

"Can you talk a little bit about the other women, and how you feel about what they all bring to the table?"

"I could talk about these women all day, so how much time do we have?" She smiles, her eyes finding mine again, and shrugs one shoulder. "They're spectacular people. Intelligent, funny, generous. It's very much been a group effort, since the beginning. We all have a say on everything, and sometimes we disagree."

"What happens if you disagree?" Trevor asks.

"We take a vote," she says. "In fact, you're here because of a majority vote."

"Really?" Trevor tips his head to the side. "Who didn't want me to come?"

"I'm not telling," Kat says, holding her hands up in surrender. "The point is, this is a team effort. We all put in double what a normal work week looks like. Sometimes we sleep here."

"Sleep here?" Trevor asks.

"Sure. If I'm here working on inventory and such into the wee hours, I just crash here. Or, I should say, I used to, before I met Mac. He prefers I go home these days."

"As he should," Trevor replies. "Can you walk me through your workday?"

Kat continues to answer Trevor's questions honestly, with humor and the love she has for our place shining through her eyes.

When she's done, we all stand to stretch and Shawn unhooks her from the sound, reaching down her clothes to get all of the wires out.

"She did great," I whisper, and take a deep breath, and suddenly Trevor turns to me and wraps his arm around my shoulders.

Holy shit, he smells good.

"Stop worrying, Riley. She was great. You're all going to be great. I promise."

I smile and nod, not able to speak. The more time I spend with him, the more attracted I am to him. And then he had to go and wear a suit today.

Shit.

He turns back to his notes, and I take another deep breath, wondering what in the hell I'm going to do with this pent-up sexual aggression and the attraction I feel for Trevor.

Maybe going out on a date tonight will take my mind off him.

I doubt it, but a girl can hope.

"Wow, YOU HAVEN'T changed at all," Dave says as he sits across the table from me. I wish I could say the same about him.

Dave and I dated for two years in high school, and he's recently moved back to town. He called last week, and we set the date for tonight.

But Dave has done nothing *but* change. In high school, he was a jock, tall and built, with dark blond hair and a killer smile.

And now he's lost a good portion of his hair, he's let himself go, and his smile just looks . . . *smarmy.*

"Thanks," I reply, and take a big sip of my wine. "What have you been up to?"

"Well, I lived in the San Francisco area for a while."

"Oh?" I sit back as the waitress delivers my food, and wait for Dave to keep talking. Maybe, if we eat really fast, this date will be over sooner rather than later. My biggest regret is that I let him pick me up, so I'll have to ride back from downtown Portland to my house with him as well.

I know better than that.

"Yep, I was down there for about eight years. Had three kids."

"Really? So you got married?" I take a bite of broccoli, but can't actually taste anything, so I set my fork back on my plate.

"Well, the third baby's mama talked me into marrying her, but that's not working out." He shrugs, and I'm taken totally aback.

"So, you're *still* married?"

"Yeah," he says, as if he's telling me that he put gas in his car before he picked me up. "But, man, she's a bitch."

"So you're going through a divorce."

He shifts in his seat and won't meet my eyes now.

"I'm sorry, Dave, I misunderstood when you called last week. I thought this was a date." I laugh and take another sip of my wine, relieved. "But I can quickly switch to friend-zone mode."

"No." He shakes his head. "This *is* a date. I wanted to see you."

I narrow my eyes and suddenly have a *very* bad feeling for what's about to go down.

"You're married."

He brushes that off. "I just need to tell her I want the divorce. I moved back up here, like I told you over the phone. I'm staying with Mom and Dad for a while because I'm still looking for a job, and all three baby mamas think I'm made of money or something, always wanting money."

Now my jaw tightens and hands clench in my lap.

"I heard that you've done well for yourself with that porn restaurant."

I'm quite sure my eyes are going to pop out of my head.

"And to be honest, I need someone who can help me out. I need to be with a girl who has her shit together, you know?"

Because you're a colossal shit show.

But I don't say anything quite yet, I just sit back and wait for him to finish his spiel about how he's lonely, and needs nine thousand dollars.

As if I have nine thousand dollars to give him.

Finally, unable to listen to him anymore, I hold up my hand to stop him.

"Stop talking." I take another sip of wine.

"I'm really a great guy. I mean, you know that."

"Shut. Up. You're a great guy? I wear heels bigger than your dick." He blinks fast, clearly shocked by that statement. But I'm just getting started.

"Let me get this straight. You have three children, all from different mothers, and you married the third. You're *still married* to her."

"Yes, but—"

"I said shut it." I glare across the table at him and he stops talking. "You're a piece of garbage, Dave. You won't financially support your children, and I may not know you anymore, but I can pretty much guess that you don't emotionally support them either."

"They're just kids—"

"And now you're living with your parents, probably avoiding the whole job thing because they'd just garnish your wages for child support."

"I'm looking for something under the table—"

"I'm so relieved that I broke up with you when I did. I dodged a *huge* bullet with you. I think you're nothing but a jackass, and all three of those children deserve far better than they'll ever get from you.

"I'm leaving now. I will not sit here and listen to this bullshit. And as far as ever getting a dime out of me, or anything else? Fuck you, Dave."

I stand and throw my napkin on the table and grab my handbag.

"I can't afford all of this," he says angrily, and I just keep on walking.

What an asshole!

And now I'm stuck in downtown Portland, late in the evening, with no car. Cabs don't just drive around here like they do in New York. You have to call for one.

But I'm *pissed off* and I want to vent.

I want to yell.

I might want to punch something.

The girls are all busy tonight with their men, Mia's at the restaurant.

But Trevor's place isn't far. I could easily walk there.

I take my phone out of my handbag and call.

"Hello."

"Hi, Trevor, it's Riley."

"Hi," he says again, "are you okay? Your voice sounds different."

"I was just wondering if you're home, and if so, can I stop in? I'm in the neighborhood."

"Sure, that's fine," he replies. "Are you sure you're okay? Do you need me to come get you?"

Stop being so fucking nice to me.

"No, it's not far. But I'm going to order a pizza, if you don't mind."

There will be an enormous amount of stress eating to-night.

"I don't mind."

"Okay." I take a deep breath. "I'll be there in a few."

I'm already walking toward his building.

Correction: I'm stomping toward his building.

Because I'm *pissed*. And not a little hurt, which just pisses me off more.

I make my way up to Trevor's place and knock on his door. When it swings open, I'm met with him wearing sweats, a T-shirt, his glasses, and a remote for something in his hand.

"Gotta go," he says quickly, "She just got here. Bye, guys."

He yanks an earbud out of one ear.

"Am I interrupting?" I ask.

"I was just playing a game," he says. "No biggie."

I nod and walk in, pacing around his tiny apartment.

"What's up, Ri?" he asks.

I shake my head, and he leans against the wall, his arms crossed over his chest, watching.

"I'm pissed off."

"I gathered that much," he says, watching me through those sexy-as-fuck glasses.

"Why are all men horrible?" I finally ask, and toss my bag on the kitchen counter. Not hard, because it's a Louis, but hard enough to be satisfying.

"In what way?"

I just roll my eyes and keep pacing. I'm getting dizzy. I hope the pizza arrives soon because I'm *starving*.

"I went out with this guy I dated in high school," I begin, and tell him the whole story, all the way through me leaving the restaurant. "I mean, what in the actual *fuck,* Trevor?"

The doorbell rings with the pizza, and I immediately run for it and fling it open.

"Thank God you're here."

The kid grins. "I wish all the pretty girls I delivered to answered the door like this."

"They don't?" I ask, and walk over to retrieve my wallet.

"Hell no." He smiles wider, then sees Trevor across the room. "Well, it's a bummer you already have a guy here."

"Huh?" I ask as I count out the money. The food smells *amazing.*

"Here," Trevor says, and shoves several bills into the kid's hands and closes the door in his face.

"It didn't cost that much."

"I don't care," Trevor growls.

"What's wrong with *you*?" I demand. "I mean, is there just a rude gene in all men that kicks in when you're around *me*? Because you were a complete asshole to that poor kid."

"Fuck that, he was flirting with you."

"Oh no, we can't have that. Not a kid, who's about ten years too young for me, by the way, flirting with me! Call the police! Call the motherfucking FBI!"

He grabs my shoulders tightly and lowers his face to mine.

"Enough!"

Chapter Four

~Trevor~

We're both panting, both riled up, and I want to shake her and kiss the fuck out of her, all at the same time. Her blue eyes are dilated, her lips wet from her pink tongue licking them, and Jesus, I want her.

"Stop this," I say, and loosen my hold on her. "Not all men are assholes."

She lets out a deep sigh and her shoulders sag. "I'm sorry. You're right. I'm taking it out on you, and it's not your fault. You weren't even there."

And that's one more thing that pisses me off. If anyone is going to take her out, it should be *me*. Not that it makes any sense, I have no claim on her, but damn it, the thought of her going out with some dickhead cuts me.

"You need to calm down and maybe eat some pizza," I say at last, and she smiles up at me softly.

"I didn't get to eat at the restaurant. I left too quickly."

"Well, we have plenty of food here." I pull down plates, also hungry, and we dish up, then sit in my living room. She's on the couch and I'm in the recliner.

"What did I interrupt?" she asks as she takes a big bite of her slice.

"I was playing Xbox online with some friends."

"Do you do that a lot? Are you a gamer?"

I grin and shrug one shoulder. "Yeah. It's okay, I'm a geek. It doesn't bother me."

"It shouldn't," she says with a frown.

"Are *you* a gamer?" I ask.

"No." She smiles. "No, I've never tried to play. Not really my thing. I just think that no one should be embarrassed about their hobbies. It's cool that you can talk to other people."

I nod and reach for another slice. "My best friend and I have played together since we were kids. We grew up together. And this is how we hang out together."

"Cool." She smiles and wipes off her mouth. "I'm sorry for going off on you."

"I'm concerned about the people you choose to go out with, Riley," I reply honestly. "They're not just guys with different interests, they're complete and utter pieces of shit."

"Boy, you're not kidding," she says. "I mean, I didn't even meet Dave online. I've known him a long time. He wasn't this big of an ass in high school."

"But he was probably still an ass, but you were young and able to overlook a lot."

"True," she replies with a thoughtful nod.

"I'm glad you were smart enough to walk out, but I don't like that you were stranded in downtown Portland alone." I finish my pizza, tossing the last few bites aside. "You could have been hurt. What if I wasn't staying so close by?"

"I would have called one of the girls to come get me," she says, like it's no big deal. "Besides, I usually drive myself."

I narrow my eyes, watching her eat. I've known her for just over a week, and I like her. I'm fucking attracted to her. But more than that, I feel possessive and protective, more than I did even when I was married. Which is crazy.

What the fuck is wrong with me? Has it just been too long since I got laid?

I immediately cast that thought aside. I'm not simply horny.

I care.

"What are you thinking?" she asks. My gaze finds hers.

"I have an idea," I reply.

"Okay."

"I'm going to take you out on a date. I'm going to show you how a woman should be treated."

She tips her head to the side. "What if I say no?"

"You can't."

She busts out laughing. "Trust me, I can say no."

"Okay, I'm hoping you won't say no. I have a fragile ego."

"I call bullshit on that as well," she says with a smile. "What do you have in mind?"

"Let me worry about the details. I'll pick you up tomorrow around four."

"I'll be at the restaurant then."

I grin and nod. "So will I."

"Convenient."

I nod and push my glasses up my nose, already forming a plan.

"What should I wear?" she asks.

Nothing at all.

"Whatever you want. We'll start out with something casual."

"Okay." She smiles. "Has anyone ever told you that the glasses are sexy?"

Many times. But I grin and shake my head no.

"Well, they are."

"So, you think I'm sexy?"

She giggles. "I didn't say that. I said the glasses are sexy."

"I think *you're* sexy," I reply honestly. "And I'm not quite sure what to do about that."

She looks taken aback for a moment, blinking quickly, but she recovers and tucks her hair behind one ear.

"Well, I guess you're taking me out on a date tomorrow, so we'll see what happens."

"This is a lot of pressure to perform well on said date."

"You're the one who suggested it," she says with a smirk. "Poor sucker."

She makes me laugh. She's dry and witty, and I never know what's going to come out of her mouth. Spending time with her, away from work and on an actual date, is going to be fun.

And I'm going to do my best to keep my hands off her. It's a first date, after all.

WE LEFT THE restaurant ten minutes ago, and my whole fucking body is on high alert. Apparently, *"casual"* means wearing black capris with red heels and a white-and-black polka-dot blouse.

The shoes are going to kill me. Dead. I didn't realize before that I had a foot or shoe fetish, but the way Riley wears them makes me want to strip her bare, aside from the shoes, wrap her legs around my shoulders, and go to town on her.

But we can't do that today.

Not that we should do that *any* day.

I park in underground parking and escort Riley up to the Portland Art Museum.

"I haven't been here in years," she says with a smile.

"And I've never been, so it should be fun."

She nods and joins me as I pay for our tickets and gather a brochure with a map of the place. I take her hand in mine as we walk inside.

"Where should we start?" I ask.

"Modern art?"

"Done." We walk into the exhibit, staring at works of art on the walls, quietly moving from one display to the next.

"I don't get this one," Riley says, tilting her head to the side. "I mean, did they hang it wrong?"

"Probably not," I reply with a smile.

"It looks like boobs," she says at last. I read the plaque beneath it.

"It says *Tulips in Spring.*"

She shrugs. "Still looks like boobs."

"Maybe modern art isn't our favorite," I suggest, and pull out the map. "European art?"

"Well, at least I can actually tell the difference between boobs and tulips in that exhibit," she says, so we head that way. For the next two hours, we make our way through the museum, studying pieces that interest us and walking past others that don't.

"I don't know how you're doing this in those shoes," I finally say.

"I live in heels," she says. "It's no biggie. I'll take them off when I get home and I'll be fine."

"Are they bothering you now?"

"Like I said, I'm fine." She pats my arm and glides her hand down to link her fingers with mine. "Thanks for checking, though."

"I'll carry them, if you want to go barefoot."

Her smile is bright. "That's sweet. But no, I don't mind."

A foot rub is on my list of things to see to later. Her face lights up when she sees a photography exhibit and she leads us over to check it out.

Throughout our time here, we've seen hundreds of pieces of art, but she's the only thing I can't stop staring at.

"I know it's early, but this is a really fun date," Riley says, taking me by surprise.

"I'm glad," I reply, and lean in to kiss her forehead. She's warm and smells like heaven.

I may not have plans to get her naked later, but there will be kissing.

This is a date.

"Are you hungry?" I ask.

"Yes."

"Good. Let's go eat. Unless there's something else you want to check out?"

"I think we've seen just about everything here," she says with smile. "I'm ready when you are."

"Let's go, then."

"So, THIS WAS a good date," Riley says later as I drive her home. She rode to work with Addie so I could take her home after our date.

"I'm glad you approve," I reply, and kiss the back of her hand. "Now, I won't be calling or texting for three days."

"Why?"

"Because that's how it's done." I sigh and shrug, as if to say, *What can I do?* Riley chuckles.

"Well, then I'll text the girls '*I hate this guy,*' and then you'll text and I'll be all, '*Never mind. He just texted.*'"

"Yes, I believe you're familiar with how this works."

"Well," she says. "I'm not really much of a drama girl. You should just go ahead and call or text whenever you want to."

"Really? *You're* not one for drama? I seem to remember someone barging into my apartment last night, yelling at me, because her date didn't go well."

"I'm only human, Trevor," she says with a smile. "I never claimed to be perfect."

I laugh as she points out her driveway and I pull in, then escort her up to her door.

"I had fun," she says.

"You sound surprised."

"Pleasantly surprised," she says. "Do you want to come in?"

"Yes," I reply, and cage her in against the door. "But I'm not going to."

She swallows hard. "You aren't?"

"No." I kiss her forehead.

"Why not?" It's a whisper now.

"Because this is the first date," I remind her, and kiss her cheek. "So I'm going to be a gentleman and say good night right here on your porch."

"Well, damn."

I grin and nudge her face up to mine, and let myself sink into her, our lips tangled. She fists her hands in my shirt at my sides, holding on tight, and giving back as good as she gets. She lifts up higher on her toes and presses her breasts to my chest, and fuck me, it's all I can do not to scoop her up, take her inside, and fuck her into the mattress.

Instead, I pull back gently, regretfully.

"Thank you for tonight," I murmur, and watch with humor as she struggles to open her eyes. The attraction is definitely not one-sided.

"Okay," she says, and touches her lips with her fingertips. "I mean, you're welcome. And thank you." She smiles, opens her door, and slips inside.

And just like that, she's gone.

But I can faintly hear her say, "Holy shit," on the other side of the door.

No, she's not immune to me either.

I whistle my way back to my car, already anticipating seeing Riley at work tomorrow.

Wait. I'm seeing Riley at *work* tomorrow. Since when have I thrown my morals out the window?

When I get home, I log into the Xbox and see Scott is already online.

"Hey, man," I say in greeting.

"How did it go?" he asks.

"It was fun."

"And?"

"I already knew that I enjoyed being with her, we've hung out before."

"Right," he says. "But I can tell that something's not right."

"This is the problem with knowing each other so long. You know everything."

He laughs. "What's up?"

"I'm more attracted to Riley than I've been to anyone in a very long time."

"That doesn't sound bad."

"I work with her."

"Well, there's that."

"If I end up pissing her off, we still have to work with each other. This is why it's a bad idea to date colleagues."

"But you're only there for a few weeks."

"And that's strike two," I reply.

"Well, you could just get naked with her while you're there. There's no need for you to be a monk."

"I don't know, man." I shake my head. Fucking her and leaving doesn't sit well with me.

"Maybe you're falling in love with her," he suggests, and I roll my eyes.

"I barely know her."

"So?"

"Why am I talking to you about this?"

"Because I'm cool," he replies. "And happily married."

"And sometimes a dipshit," I add, making him laugh.

"You're the one having second thoughts about getting naked with a hot blonde. Who's the dipshit?"

"We're both dipshits," I reply, and see my phone light up with a text.

Riley: I'm just going to get rid of the whole three-day nonsense now. I had a good time tonight. I have plans tomorrow night, but let me cook for you Saturday night?

"Where did you go?" Scott asks.

"She texted," I mutter, and reply.

Sounds great. Wait. Do you know how to cook?

"I can let you go," Scott says. "Maybe she wants you to go back to her place now."

"Don't be an asshole."

Yes, I can cook. I'll even prove it to you.

I smirk.

I don't know, can I trust you?

"Dude, go talk to your girl. You're ignoring me. I don't want to listen to dead air."

"I'm done."

Trust me. I won't kill you.

I set the phone aside and direct my attention back to Scott and killing the bad guys in our game.

"When are you going to see her again?"

"I'll see her at work tomorrow."

"That's not what I mean."

"She's making me dinner the day after tomorrow."

"You guys eat a lot."

I frown. "What else are we supposed to do? I took her to the museum today. What do you and your wife do together?"

"I guess we eat a lot."

"Exactly."

"We also have sex."

I grimace. "I don't need the details of that."

"I'm just saying."

"Let's talk about something else."

"Okay, I don't know if I should tell you this or not, but when I got home from work today, your ex was here chatting it up with Wendy."

"Okay." I frown. "What was my ex doing with your wife?"

"They stopped talking when I walked in, but it seemed harmless. I mean, we already knew that they stayed friendly."

"Did she ask about me at all?"

"No. When was the last time you heard from her?"

"More than a year ago. We don't have much drama between us. Unless she was there to get information about me, I'm not going to worry about it."

"Good call. What else is going on?" he asks, and I begin telling him about the new *Star Wars* movie trailer I saw today. We spend several hours playing and talking, until we both decide we're tired and sign off for the night.

Riley never texted again, but I didn't expect her to.

I've never regretted not staying with a woman after a date the way I do tonight. But it was the right thing to do.

I just can't guarantee that I'll be so gentlemanly next time. In fact, I know I won't be. The attraction is mutual, and we're consenting adults.

I just hope it doesn't hit the fan at work.

Chapter Five

~Riley~

*L*andon is all for the tattoo," Cami informs us Friday night. We're all gathered at Addie's house, dressed in loungewear, drinking our poison of choice.

Mine is lemon drops.

"Where do you want to put it again?" Kat asks, and sips her red wine.

"On my side, over my ribs," Cami replies, and smiles. "It's gonna hurt like a motherfucker, but it'll be sexy when it's done."

"My foot hurt like hell," I inform them all. "But also worth it."

"What does Trevor think of your ink and piercings?" Addie asks, and sips her lemon drop. "Holy shit, this is good. The only thing I hated about being pregnant was not being able to drink once in a while."

"Aren't you breastfeeding?" Mia asks.

"Yeah, but I pumped before you guys got here, so she has plenty to eat, and I'll pump when we're done to get this out of my system. I have it all figured out."

"Atta girl," Mia says, and offers her a fist to bump. "Back to you, Ri. What does Trevor think of your rebellious body art?"

I grin and sip my drink. "He hasn't seen it yet."

"What the—?" Addie's eyes are round in surprise. "You guys haven't gotten naked yet? He looks at you like he wants to eat you with a spoon."

A little shiver makes its way through me in agreement. He *totally* looks at me like he wants to eat me with a spoon. I want him to. I really, really want him to.

"It's complicated," I reply.

"Have you kissed?"

A mental image of Trevor pressing me against my front door, kissing me like he depended on it, pops into my head and the shiver isn't so little this time.

"Oh yeah."

"So what's the problem?" Cami asks.

I gulp down the rest of my drink and lean over to the coffee table to pour more. I am going to need the liquid courage to get through this conversation.

And I *need* to have this conversation.

"He took me out on a date last night," I inform them, and lick the sugar off the rim of my glass. "I'm seriously addicted to sugar. This is a problem."

"Hey, get back to the date," Cami says.

"It was nice. He said he needed to take me out so he could show me how a gentleman should behave on a date."

"Good," Cami says with a nod. "Because you've met some douche canoes since you and what's-his-name broke up."

"Where did he take you?" Kat asks, clearly avoiding the whole let's-talk-about-your-shitty-past-with-men thing.

"To the art museum, and then dinner." I smile, remembering the modern art exhibit. I hated the art in there, but being with Trevor made it so fun. "And then he took me home and kissed me on the porch and said good night."

"Wow," Addie says, and takes a long sip of her drink. "Men still do that shit?"

"This man does," I reply. "I like it. I like the tradition of it, you know? One of the things that I've *hated* about dating is that everyone is in such a hurry to fuck. And don't get me wrong, I love a good fucking as much as the next girl."

"And that's my cue that I came in at the wrong time," Jake, Addie's husband, says, and turns around to flee the room, making us all laugh.

"I guess I've been so disappointed by the lack of respect in the men I've dated."

"Trust me, I get it," Addie says with a nod. "I think we've all been there."

"Absolutely," Mia adds. "When are you going to see him again?"

"I offered to cook for him tomorrow night." I shrug and

stare at my toes. I need a pedicure. I can't have sex with Trevor until I've had these talons taken care of.

"Great, you can bone him on the second date," Kat says with a Cheshire cat smile.

"He's not permanent," I remind them.

"So?" Cami and Kat say in unison.

"So, I don't think a fling is really my thing. I mean, I don't have anything against it morally, I just don't think I'm wired that way."

"You're an old-fashioned kind of girl," Cami says with a romantic sigh and goofy smile on her face. "That's sweet."

"For all we know, Trevor doesn't want a fling either," Addie says, tapping her finger on her lips.

"You have pretty lips," I tell her, making her grin.

"The liquor kicked in," she replies. "But thanks."

It really has kicked in. My lips are a little tingly and I feel really . . . *good.*

"So, do you know what Trevor wants?" Cami asks.

"No, but I could text him." I pull my phone out of my pocket and smile when I see his name on my screen. "Aw, he already texted me."

Looking forward to dinner tomorrow night.

"Oh lord, she's smitten," Mia says with a roll of the eyes. "She's all aflutter over there."

"I'm going to ask him if he wants a fling or something serious."

"NO!" they all yell in unison.

"Absolutely not," Kat says, and dives for my phone. "Why am I always saving you bitches from embarrassing yourselves over text?"

"Good communication is important," I remind her with a frown.

"Yeah, but this isn't that. Asking him if he wants a fling is a conversation best had in person."

"Fine," I reply with a sigh. "But he texted me first, so I should reply."

She reluctantly gives me back my phone and I take a sip of my drink.

"These are really delicious. I know what I'll say! I'll tell him his glasses are sexy."

"That's a good one," Cami says with a nod. "They really are sexy."

Your glasses are sexy as fuck.

I hit send and sit back with satisfaction.

"You know," Addie says, a thoughtful look on her face. "Starting something with Trevor doesn't mean that it has to end when he leaves."

"She's right," Kat says just as Trevor's reply to my text arrives.

Your ass is sexy as fuck.

"He likes my ass," I announce, and quickly reply to him.

You should send me a selfie. I want to see you.

"I'm serious," Kat continues, "I mean, sure it's not ideal, but L.A. is only a three-hour plane ride from here."

"Says the girl who hates to fly," Cami adds with a snort. "Oh, I'm so drunk."

"Just because I don't like to fly doesn't mean that Ri can't fly to get some action."

I nod, pondering what she's saying. Trevor shoots me another text. It's a selfie of him in his glasses, sitting in his apartment. He has his nose scrunched up. "Aw, look."

The girls just smile at me while I take a selfie for him, making sure he can see my cleavage, and send it back.

"Concentrate, drunk girl," Kat says. "What about a long-distance thing?"

"That just seems like so much work," I reply. "I mean, it's hard enough to have a relationship with someone in person. Being far away would suck."

"Well, I don't mean to brag, but we're doing pretty okay for ourselves," Addie reminds me. "And I would bet that he does well too. It's not out of the realm of possibilities that you could travel to see each other on the weekends."

"Plus, he travels a lot for his job anyway," Mia adds. "It would be exciting to meet up with him in different cities."

Beautiful, as always.

Trevor's text makes me grin.

I liked it when you took me to see boobs. And kissed me.
Lots of kisses.

I hit send and return my attention to the girls. "I should just ask him if that sounds good to him. I mean, I'm drunk and all, but it sounds okay to me."

"Do *not* ask him that," Kat says sternly, and because I'm afraid she'll take away my phone again, I bite my lip and smile innocently.

Um . . . Have you been drinking?

I snort and cover my mouth with my hand, staring at all eight of the girls.

There are two of each of them.

"He asked me if I'm drunk." I smirk and find my Snapchat app. "Time for a video."

"Oh God," Mia says, hanging her head in her hand. "Girls are so dumb when they're drunk."

"It's *funny*," I reply, and find the baby bunny filter.

"Hi," I say, and let out a little giggle. "I might be drunk. Allegedly. I have a magic martini glass that keeps filling up." I cuddle the glass to my face just as my ten seconds are up, save it to my phone, and send it to Trevor.

"So, what you guys are saying is, just because he doesn't live here doesn't mean I can only have a fling with him."

"Exactly," Addie says, and raises her glass in a toast. "If you care about each other, you can figure it out."

"I guess you're right," I reply with a nod, and smile when Trevor texts back.

Okay, that's cute. Glad you're having fun. Are you safe?

"Okay, look at this." I show them his text and feel my insides go all gooey. "He's so sweet."

"That is pretty sweet. That's something Jake, Mac, or Landon would say because they love us," Cami says with a nod. "Oh, I'm so happy for you."

"Don't cry," I demand as Cami's eyes well up with tears. "Don't you dare, or I will too."

"It's just, you've waited so long to find someone who isn't a dick," she says, and sniffs loudly. "If you feel something real for this guy, you *have* to give it a try, Ri. Good guys are almost extinct."

"She's right," Mia says. "I hate to admit that, because you all know I'm sort of not the biggest fan of the male species, but if it feels right, go for it. And not just for the sex, but for the whole package. You never know, it might all be a moot point anyway. You might hate him by Monday."

"There's the cynic we all know and love," Kat says, hugging Mia around the shoulders.

"She's sort of right," I reply. "Maybe the sex will suck." I frown. "Why would I wish that on myself? The sex will definitely *not* suck. But something could happen that puts a stop to all of it anyway. Might as well see how it goes."

"Cautiously optimistic," Cami says with a slow nod. "A good way to go into it."

"Plus," I add, "have you guys seen his glasses? And his *hands*. Holy shit, he hasn't gotten me naked yet, and he already does amazing things with his hands."

"So, he's handsy," Addie says, making us laugh. "I love that word. '*Handsy*.'"

"I love a handsy man," Kat says with a grin. "As long as it's not creepy handsy."

"True," I say with a nod. "And he's not creepy at all. A little geeky." I laugh when I remember his love of *Star Wars* and video games.

"Geeks are sexy," Kat says. "Nothing wrong with that."

"Not wrong with that at all," I agree.

"WHY HAVEN'T WE had sex back here?" Cami asks Landon later as he gives us a ride home. Well, he's giving *me* a ride home and taking Cami to their home.

Because they're married.

"Seriously," she continues. "There's plenty of room."

"I'll put it on the list," Landon mutters with a grin.

"You love her," I say.

"Of course I do," he says, smiling at me.

"Even when she wants to ride in the backseat because this is a new car and she hasn't ridden back there yet," I add.

"She's fun," he says with a shrug.

Trevor is fun.

"I want to talk to Trevor," I announce, and dial his number, smiling when he answers on the second ring. "Hi, sexiest man alive."

"Well, hi there," he says.

"Oh my God, Riley, hang the phone up," Landon says in exasperation.

"No." I frown at him.

"Who was that?" Trevor asks.

"Just Landon," I reply, and wave him off, as if he can see

me. "I wanted to tell you again that I loved it when you took me to see the boobs."

"Who the fuck is that?" Landon demands.

"It's Trevor," I reply in frustration. "Stop interrupting."

"Why are you with Landon?" Trevor asks.

"Because he's driving us to my house," I reply. "Don't worry, Landon and I haven't ever had sex. Yet."

Cami snorts in the backseat and Landon glares at me, but I just think it's hilarious.

"He's taking you to your house?" Trevor asks.

"Yep."

"Oh God, I might have to throw up," Cami says.

"Sorry, I gotta go." I hang up the phone and turn in my seat to look at Cami. "You should have ridden up here! I told you that you get motion sick in the back."

"It's pretty back here," she says, and holds her stomach. "But I don't feel so good."

"Hold on, baby," Landon says, watching her in the rear-view mirror. "We're almost there, and then you can get in the front."

"Okay."

Just a few minutes later, we pull into my driveway.

And Trevor is waiting for us.

"Wow, he got here fast," I say with a frown. "Wait, did I invite him over?"

"Who is this guy?" Landon asks.

"The TV guy," Cami reminds him just as Trevor reaches my door, opens it, and reaches in to pull me out.

"Hi," I say with a grin, but when I look up into his face, he just looks . . . mad. "What did I do?"

"You tell me," he says. Landon has circled the car and comes to stand with us.

"Landon, this is Trevor." I introduce them. "I've known Landon for a long time."

Something's wrong. Trevor is tense, his jaw tight, his hands clenched.

And he's not touching me at all.

I don't like that.

"Landon," Cami says as she gets out of the backseat. "Let's go. You promised me drunk sex, remember?"

"Cami?" Trevor says, surprised. "You're with Cami?"

"Of course," I say. "I was with all of the girls. Landon is taking us home."

"I get to have sex with him," Cami says with a smile as Landon wraps her in his arms. "Because I married him."

Landon whispers something to Cami and she nods. "She's fine. Trevor's nice."

"Okay." Landon pats me on the shoulder. "Call if you need anything."

"Go get your drunk sex," I say, and wave them off. Trevor walks me to my door.

"I didn't realize he was Cami's husband," Trevor says.

"Well, you should use your super Jedi mind tricks to figure it out, big boy." I snort-laugh as I unlock the door. "It's pretty fun that you like all the geeky stuff."

"It is?"

"Yeah." I nod and turn to him. "Are you going to kiss me good night again?"

His lips twitch as he watches me with those amazing green eyes and I lean into him.

And then the porch begins to spin.

"Whoa."

"Easy there, drunk girl." He lifts me effortlessly into his arms and carries me inside. "Where's your bedroom?"

I point to the back of the house and lay my head on his shoulder. "You smell good."

He kisses my head, and I feel so safe. So pampered. I can't remember the last time a guy picked me up.

I don't know if I've ever dated a guy strong enough to pick me up and carry me.

That's kind of sad.

I've dated pussies.

I smirk and press my face to his neck.

"What's so funny?"

"I shouldn't tell you. I'm drunk."

"Maybe you *should* tell me while you're drunk."

I lean back so I can look at his face, blinking slowly. "I don't know what to do about you. And I love it that you're strong enough to carry me."

"I guess I should continue to hit the gym, then, huh?"

I grin and tuck my face back into his neck and breathe him in. He sits on my bed, still cradling me close.

Being held is fucking amazing.

"Spinning," I whisper.

"Can you stay awake long enough for me to change your clothes?"

"Mm."

And then I'm out, immediately dreaming about a naked Trevor, stripping me out of my clothes and kissing me. Holding me.

Loving me.

I STRETCH UNDER my soft sheets and frown. I feel fucking horrible.

Ugh.

I'm never drinking again.

I used to be able to drink all night and work all day, no hangover in sight. But now that I'm thirty, well, that's a thing of the distant past.

I brush my hair off my face and realize that I'm wearing a T-shirt that doesn't belong to me.

I don't wear anything to bed.

Why am I wearing something in bed?

I sit straight up and look down. Nope, not my shirt.

Fuck me.

I grab my phone and call Cami. She answers, but I can tell I woke her.

I don't fucking care.

"What did you let me do?" I ask with a loud whisper.

"Huh?"

I hear rustling in my kitchen.

"I think someone is in my house," I say, my heart rate up

and panic starting to set in. "Who the fuck is in my house, Cami? How could you let me bring someone home? I mean, we didn't have sex because I'm not sore. If we *did* have sex, he has the tiniest dick in the history of dicks, and if I had sex with that, I'll never admit it. You can't tell anyone."

"Jesus, stop rambling," she says just as my bedroom door opens and I drop the phone with a scream, then stare at Trevor.

A shirtless, rumpled, sleepy Trevor who's holding a serving tray.

I have a serving tray?

"Riley?" Cami is calling through the phone. I pick it up, my eyes still clinging to his.

"Sorry. It's Trevor. Go back to sleep."

I hang up and pull the covers up to my chin as Trevor sets the tray on the nightstand and sits next to me, tucking my hair behind my ear.

"Good morning," he says with a sexy smile. My eyes keep drifting down to his smooth skin and sculpted muscles.

"Morning," I reply with a whisper. "I had no idea you looked like that under your clothes."

He smirks and my eyes find his again.

"I had no idea you had that ink under your clothes," he replies, and I feel my eyes go wide. "We'll have to talk about that sometime."

"How did you see my ink? Did we—"

"No," he says, shaking his head. "I don't have the smallest dick in the history of dicks."

"Oh, good."

He laughs and holds a glass of something gross in front of me.

"No thanks."

"Drink it," he insists. "It'll help with the hangover."

"I'm not hungover."

He takes my chin in his fingers and raises my gaze to his. "No lying. Ever. Tell me what I don't want to hear, but don't lie to me."

"Okay, I don't want that shit, I want coffee."

He nods toward the tray.

"I brought some of that too, but drink this first. It really does help."

"How did I get this T-shirt on?" I ask as I take the glass and eye it dubiously. It's green. And there are chunks in it. I take a sip and scowl.

"Drink it fast," he says with a grin.

"You're enjoying this."

"Immensely."

I gulp half the glass down, then shove it back at him. "Enough. Hand over the coffee."

"Good girl," he says, and passes me a steaming cup of coffee, black.

Just the way I like it.

"I put my shirt on you last night. I don't know where you keep your things, and you couldn't sleep in your clothes."

"I'm still in my bra and panties."

He nods. "The first time I see you completely bare, you'll be conscious and a willing partner."

"Sounds fair." I offer him a small smile, already starting to feel better. "The coffee is working."

"It's my smoothie," he says with confidence. "You're beautiful in the morning."

"Oh, I can just imagine how I must look right now," I reply. "I'm sorry."

"Why?"

"This isn't how I envisioned our first morning together."

He just smiles and passes me some toast. "Did you have fun last night?"

I nod and take a bite. "We try to do a girls' night about once a month. Catch up, laugh, drink."

"Let off some steam," he says.

"Pretty much." I finish one half of the toast and take the other half. "This is nice."

"What's that?"

"Having someone here to help me feel better," I admit, and duck my head. "Silly, huh?"

"Not at all." He drags his knuckles down my cheek. "I bet a shower will help you feel better too."

I wrinkle my nose. "Yes. I'm quite sure I stink. We might have to burn this shirt when I'm finished with it."

"I think that's a bit extreme," he says with a laugh. "You don't smell bad."

"No lying." I throw his words back at him.

"Okay, you don't smell *horrible*."

I smirk and throw the covers back. "Okay, to the shower I go. I'd invite you, but this isn't going to be pretty."

"Next time," he says. The tone of his voice has me turn

back to look at him. He's watching me with the eyes of a predator. He wants me.

Thank God.

But the conversation from last night comes back to me. *What*, exactly, does he want? I'm not sure, but I don't think a guy who's interested in a quick fuck would spend the time taking care of me this morning.

It's a conversation we should have.

Later.

After I've had a shower and pulled myself together.

Chapter Six

~Trevor~

Riley is the most fascinating person I've ever met. And I've met a lot of very interesting people.

I'm on my way back to her place after I ran home to quickly shower, change, and gather a few things to throw in my car in case I end up spending the night with her.

I really fucking hope she lets me stay with her.

Keeping my hands off her has become the challenge of the year. Even this morning, when she stared at me through her tousled hair, her makeup smudged on her face, I wanted to tuck her under me and fuck her all day long. My hormones are working overtime lately.

What the fuck is happening to me?

I pull into her driveway and walk inside without knocking, per her request earlier.

"Riley?" I call out.

"In the kitchen," she replies, and smiles at me as I turn the corner to find her. "I'm getting a head start on food."

"It's only three," I remind her, and stare in horror at the mess she's already made.

"I know, but I want the sauce to simmer for a bit." She points to a stool on the other side of the island. "Sit. Watch."

"I can help."

"No." She shakes her head vigorously. "I can do this."

"What are you making?"

She finishes chopping an onion. I'm relieved because I expected her to chop off her finger any second.

"Spaghetti."

"From scratch?"

"Well, the pasta isn't from scratch. Don't tell Mia."

I rest my chin in my hand, leaning on the bar, so I can just sit and watch her move about her space. "Your secret is safe with me."

"I am making the sauce from scratch. It's almost ready to simmer."

"Awesome."

"You're making me nervous," she announces.

"Why?"

"Because you really know how to do all of this and I'm not great at it."

I shrug. "You're doing great."

"Talk. That'll make me feel less like you're judging every move I make."

"What would you like me to talk about?"

She measures the tomato sauce and shrugs. "Tell me about your family."

"Well, I told you about my sisters."

"Do you have any brothers?"

"No, it's just the three of us."

She nods and scratches her cheek, leaving a red streak of sauce there.

She's fucking adorable.

"Parents still married?"

"No. Yours?"

"My dad passed away when I was a teenager. Mom re-married six months later."

"That was quick."

"She was lonely. I'm an only child, and Mom's one of those people who just *can't* be alone, you know? She would never cheat on her husband. But she doesn't do well single. So it didn't surprise her family at all when she got married right away."

"My ex was like that," I reply with a nod. "She was en-gaged to marry someone else before the ink was dry on our divorce. Also, she *did* cheat on me, so she was different in that regard."

"That sucks," Riley says with a frown. "I don't get the whole cheating thing. I mean, if you want to fuck around with other people, just leave the relationship you're already in."

"I think that for her, she enjoyed the secrets. Like, it was a game to her to see how long she could go until I caught her."

"And how long did she go?"

"About two months," I reply, and nod when Riley holds up a bottle of water. "I would have caught her sooner, but I was already traveling a lot for my job."

"And let me guess," Riley says, "she said she was lonely because you were gone so much."

"Of course." I take a swig of water. "Apparently, I was taking too long to figure it out because I came home from the airport one evening and they were fucking in my bed."

"Ouch," she says with a cringe. "Not cool."

"Not cool," I agree.

"Did you punch him? Did she cry and tug on your arm while she clutched the sheet to her breasts and begged you to understand?"

I lean back and laugh, delighted with Riley. God, she's a breath of fresh air.

"No, nothing that dramatic."

"Damn."

She turns away, her hips swaying back and forth to a tune in her head as she pulls the refrigerator door open and stares inside, looking for something. Her hair is up in a messy bun, she's wearing black yoga pants and an oversized pink T-shirt that falls off one shoulder.

I've never wanted to kiss a shoulder so bad in my life.

"What *did* happen?" she asks from inside the fridge.

"I waited for them to see me, then turned and walked out without a word."

"Wow," she says, and stirs her sauce. "That's telling."

"How so?"

"Well, if you were deeply in love with her, you would have been devastated when you found her bumping uglies with the other dude. To walk away calmly tells me that you weren't that invested."

"Interesting." I take another sip of water, thinking about her theory. "I believed I loved her."

"Being in love and loving someone are two very different things," she says. "Did she protest when you told her you wanted a divorce?"

"No." I shake my head and push my glasses up my nose. "We agreed that it was time to go our own ways."

"So, no fights? No hard feelings?"

"We didn't really fight," I reply, wondering why this subject isn't making me very uncomfortable with Riley. "I wasn't excited about paying her alimony for three years, but aside from that, it was pretty low-key."

"And she's remarried?"

"Yep, to the dude she was fucking in my bed. It's their bed now."

"That's weird," she says, scrunching up her face. "I mean, I would *not* want to keep a bed that my guy had sex with his wife in. Does that make sense?"

"Absolutely. That's why I let her have it."

"I'm sorry that happened to you."

"I'm not," I reply honestly.

Her head comes up in surprise. "You're not?"

"No. Divorce was inevitable. We just didn't work well

as a partnership. We wanted different things, had different philosophies."

"You're very grown up," she says, tilting her head to the side the way she does that makes me want to pull her to me and kiss the hell out of her. "I like that about you."

I chuckle as I stand and walk over to where she's stirring her sauce. She takes a taste off her spoon, then holds it up for me to taste as well.

But rather than take it from the spoon, I lean in and kiss her. Thoroughly. She's soft, and willing and so fucking sweet. She leans into me just as I take the spoon from her hand and lay it down, then pull her into my arms, enjoying the way her body fits against mine.

When I finally pull back, I smile down into her face and drag my fingertips down her cheek. "It tastes delicious."

"What does?"

Her eyes are hooded, and she licks her lips, still holding on to me.

"The sauce."

"What sauce?"

I kiss her forehead and then her lips again. "The sauce you made for us."

"Oh, right." She nudges her nose against mine. "I don't care about the sauce."

"I do." I hug her tightly, and then pull away. "I'm hungry."

"Me too, but it isn't for spaghetti," she mutters as she returns to stirring the sauce. "So you and your ex are still friendly?"

"Talking about my ex isn't exactly what I like to do when I'm thinking about kissing you," I inform her, and lean my hips on the counter.

"I'm trying to slow my roll here," she says with a laugh. "So just humor me."

"We're on good terms, yes."

"But you're not weird like Cami, right?"

"How is Cami weird?"

"She's not only on good terms with her ex, she's pretty much besties with him. And she tried to set him up with all of us. She cares about him, but knew they shouldn't be married. She felt so guilty, she just wanted him to find happiness."

"Never heard that one before," I say, rubbing my fingers over my lips. "No, I'm not friends with her like that. Unless we have business stuff to talk about, like alimony payments or paperwork, we don't really speak."

"Are you friends on Facebook?" she asks, her eyes narrowed.

"No," I reply. "And I'm rarely on there anyway."

She nods thoughtfully. "Okay, it sounds normal."

"What about you? Are you still besties with all of your exes?"

"I've never been married," she replies with a frown.

"Boyfriends?"

"Well, clearly Dave and I aren't friends," she says while rolling her eyes. "I mean, ew. No, I'm not friends with anyone I've ever dated in the past. I just think it's weird when it's over. I'm not really jealous, I just don't want to know. You know?"

"I do."

"Are you hungry?" she asks. "I can start the pasta now if you are."

"Oh, I'm hungry," I reply, and watch as she glances up and her eyes widen. "I don't know if I've ever been this hungry."

She frowns, and I immediately know that I've said the wrong thing.

"Are we not on the same page, Ri? Because you've been sending out some pretty strong sexy signals."

"We're on the same page," she says, and pours pasta into boiling water. "I wanted to text you about this last night when I was drunk but Kat wouldn't let me."

"Probably not a good idea," I agree, and take her hand in mine, linking our fingers. "What's up?"

"So—" She bites her lip and looks down. Her cheeks are flushed.

"No need to be embarrassed."

"I'm not," she says, and wrinkles her nose. "Maybe I could text it to you *now*. It would be easier."

"It's like a Band-Aid, babe, just say it."

"I just . . ." She rolls her eyes and lets out a long sigh. "Jesus, I'm a grown-ass woman. Okay, here's the thing: I don't do flings."

"Okay."

"I mean, I don't judge those who do. My friends have in the past, and I don't have an issue with that. To each their own."

"Right."

"But for *me*"—she points at her chest—"I don't like it."

She sighs as if she's just admitted to committing murder.

"No flings." I nod once. "Got it."

"Do you?" She's staring up at me with pleading eyes now. "Do you get what I'm saying?"

"I was hoping there was more to this explanation," I reply.

"Okay. The one-night stand, or short-term fuck-buddy thing doesn't interest me."

"Well, when you put it like that, it doesn't interest me either."

"And you don't live here."

Ah.

"You're right. I don't."

"So, I guess the point of all of this is, I don't know what you want." She holds her hands up in frustration. "If you just want a fuck buddy for while you're working in Portland, I'm not your girl. And I'm not saying we have to get married next week, because that's just crazy."

"But there should be something in between," I finish for her, and she smiles softly.

"Exactly."

"Well, let me say this. I don't know where this might go later, but I am not simply interested in fucking you and leaving in a few weeks without looking back. You intrigue me, Riley, and this hasn't happened in a very long time for me."

"It's complicated," she says. "We live in different cities and you travel a lot."

"Yes, geography isn't on our side," I reply with a smile. I reach out and cup her cheek in my palm. "I am not psychic.

I don't know how either of us will feel in a few weeks. I do know that today I'm enjoying your company very much. You make me laugh, you make me think. And you make me so fucking horny my teeth ache."

"Those are all nice things," she whispers.

"So no, I don't want a fling either. I want to get to know you better."

"That would be nice."

I grin and lean in to brush my lips over hers. "And I think our sex timeline just changed."

"What? Why?" Her eyes widen again in panic.

"Because this isn't a sprint, sweetheart. It's a marathon. There's no hurry."

"Damn it," she grumbles, and loads our plates full of steaming food. "Okay. I guess we can just eat, then. Can we at least make out later?"

"Well, duh."

I FUCKING *HATE* today. It's Monday, and everything that can possibly go wrong, is. Not to mention stuff I haven't even thought about.

"What the fuck!" Mia exclaims as she surveys the delivery that just arrived. "I don't have any of the ingredients I special-ordered for filming today."

"Sorry, ma'am," the delivery guy says, "someone screwed up and didn't include it. I won't have it for you until tomorrow."

"That's not okay," Mia replies. I'm pretty sure that if looks could kill, this dude would be in big trouble.

"There's nothing I can do," he says with a shrug, and turns to leave.

"Jesus," she whispers, pinching the bridge of her nose. "I guess I can just go to the grocery store to buy the stuff, but it's a pain in the ass."

"We're already behind on filming," I remind her. Thanks to the lights blowing up this morning when they were dropped, I've had to send people out to buy new bulbs.

"I can't make the food magically appear," she says, turning her glare on me.

"Clearly not," I reply, and shove my hand through my hair. "We'll film it tomorrow."

"Great." She tosses a pan across the room to the sink. "I get to put this disgusting makeup on again tomorrow."

"Not my fault your delivery people fucked up," I reply, and brace myself for a fight just as Riley walks through the door.

"Listen to me, asshole," Mia begins.

"Hey," Riley says, standing between us. "What's up?"

"He's pissing me off," Mia says.

"Let's take a break." Riley pulls me out of the kitchen by the arm and leads me to her office. She shuts the door behind us. "What's going on?"

"This is a motherfucker of a day," I reply, and sit in a chair heavily. "Lights broke, sound isn't working right, the food wasn't delivered. Everyone is in a bad freaking mood."

"Including you," she says, earning a stare from me.

"Not to mention I got a fantastic lecture from my boss

this morning because losing even one day of filming costs the network money."

"It happens," she replies. She's not mocking me, she's being exactly what I need right now: the calm in the storm.

"It's a Monday."

"Maybe you should call it a day," she suggests, and cups my cheek in her hand, smiling down at me. I reach out and tug her into my lap so I can hug her close. She smells like vanilla.

"You feel great."

She kisses the top of my head. "It's all going to be okay, Trevor. Call it a day for now, regroup, and try again tomorrow."

"That won't make my boss any less pissed."

"Turn the sound off on your phone. You're the man on the ground, and you're here doing your job. Obviously, they trust your judgment. When will you have new lights?"

"Tomorrow. And the food will be here tomorrow as well."

"See? You can't do any more today."

I lean back so I can look up into her beautiful face. She's brushing the hair out of my eyes.

"Thank you."

"For what?" she asks.

"For being you." I kiss her softly and stand with her still in my arms. She gets a kick out of it when I lift her, so I find myself doing it often.

"I'm kicking you out of here," she says.

"You're not the boss of me."

"I beg to differ," she says, and kisses me long and slow. "Go home. Play a game, or take a nap. Take the day off."

"You should come do that with me."

She smiles. "I would love to, but I have a few things to do here, and then I have to run home to meet the plumber."

"What are you having fixed now?"

"I have a leak in my bathroom."

I set her on her feet gently. "I can come with you."

"No." She shakes her head firmly. "Go home. I've got this. Maybe I'll come over later."

She drags her finger down the front of my shirt, over the buttons. We spent the weekend together, except when she went out for brunch with the girls on Sunday. I love her company. I crave it.

I crave her.

"I'd like for you to come over later," I reply, and kiss her forehead.

"Done," she says. "I won't even ask you to go make nice with Mia."

"I'm ninety-nine percent sure she's going to take a hit out on me."

"Nah," Riley says with a laugh. "Any killing Mia does, she does it herself." She winks and makes me laugh.

"You're good for me," I reply earnestly.

"I hope so," she says. "Now go let your guys off the hook for today, and I'll see you later."

"Yes, ma'am."

I shouldn't take today off. There is a ton of work to do, but Riley's right. The correct equipment won't be here until tomorrow morning. If I ask everyone to stay, they'll just sit around and be pissy.

Even I don't want to deal with that.

So I do what Riley suggests and send everyone home for the day, then make my way back to the apartment myself. It's quiet here. Too quiet. So I turn the game system on, but I can't play with Scott at this time of day because he's still at work. I'll just work on some single-player stuff this afternoon.

But my eyes are heavy, and my brain is too full to concentrate on the game.

So I peel out of my clothes and go to bed, wishing Riley was curled up next to me.

Chapter Seven

~Riley~

He's not answering his phone. I don't know if that means I should *not* go to his place, or maybe I should be worried because he fell and hit his head and now he's bleeding out in his kitchen.

Too many thriller movies lately, Riley.

I smirk and approach his door, juggling my packages as I knock, but he doesn't answer. So I knock again.

Where in the hell is he? He didn't text to say that something else came up. He's not the type to just blow me off.

At least, I don't think he is.

Maybe he really is, but he was just hiding it before.

What an ass. I snarl at the door, flip it off, and turn to stomp down the hallway to the elevator.

"Wait!"

Trevor's voice stops me, and I turn to find him standing

in his doorway, rubbing his eyes, and clinging precariously to a towel that's wrapped around his waist.

I'm quite sure he's naked beneath it.

Christ on a cracker, I wish that towel would fall. My eyes travel up his naked torso, over the smooth skin, light spattering of brown hair, and to the smirk parked on his handsome face.

"Hi." My voice squeaks, of course, so I clear my throat and try again. "Hello."

"Leaving so soon?"

"You weren't answering," I reply. "I thought you'd blown me off."

All humor leaves his face and he tilts his head to the side, frowning at me.

"Let's get something straight right now, Riley. I'm not an asshole, and I definitely wouldn't blow you off. I fell asleep."

And just like that, all of my indignation evaporates.

"Sorry." I walk to him and rise up on my tiptoes to kiss his cheek. "I brought provisions."

"Dinner?" he asks.

"Better." I walk past him into the apartment and set the bag on the countertop. "Cupcakes and *Star Wars*."

His eyes widen with interest. "You don't say."

"I do say," I reply with a flirty smile. "I figured it was time that I watch this dude movie, and I should watch it with someone who truly appreciates it."

"Agreed," he replies, and leans in to kiss me gently. "Thank you."

"I'm handy."

"Very handy," he agrees, and kisses my cheek now. "Run away with me, Ri."

I giggle and try to slip away, but he wraps his arms around me, not caring in the least that he's just let go of his towel, effectively letting it fall to our feet.

"You're irresistible," he murmurs in my ear.

"You're just smelling the cupcakes." I giggle and lean into him, enjoying his playful touch.

"The cupcakes are a close second," he says, and pulls away. "I'm going to put on some clothes real quick. Don't go away."

He retrieves his towel, but doesn't bother wrapping it around him, and I have a prime view of his perfect ass, including the dimples above the cheeks, and his sculpted back as he walks away to the bedroom.

"Fuck me," I breathe, and fan my face. Part of me wants to run after him, tackle him to the bed, and have my wicked way with him.

Do it!

But he's fast, because just as I'm about to chase him down, he returns wearing an old T-shirt and a pair of basketball shorts.

And still manages to look sexier than my hormones can handle.

How does he do that?

"Do I have something on my shirt?" he asks, looking down.

"No." I shake my head and turn back to the cupcakes. "Sorry. So, Mia made these today. She bakes when she's too stressed out. She sent them with me as a peace offering."

"Well, I won't say she shouldn't have because those look amazing."

"You have no idea," I reply with a wink. "Here's the movie."

He takes it from me and walks into the small living room to cue it up.

"Where did you get this?" he asks.

"It's Landon's," I reply. "He was just as shocked as you when I told him I hadn't seen it before."

"Well, we're going to fix that."

I set the cupcakes on the coffee table and we both sit on the couch, cuddled up to each other. It's amazing how I just fit into the crook of his shoulder. His arm is draped down my back, hand resting on my hip as the movie starts.

He reaches for a cupcake, peels back the paper and takes a bite, then offers me a bite, which I happily take.

"Oh my God," I say, my mouth full. "So good."

I glance up at him, and he's watching me intently through those glasses, his green eyes on fire.

"What?"

"Say that again, and we won't make it through this movie."

"No?"

"No. I'll fuck you right here on the couch."

And just like that, my panties are soaked and a shiver runs down my spine.

"That's not exactly a horrible threat," I whisper, watching his lips. They tip up on one side with a sexy grin.

"I really want you to see this."

"I really want to see it too."

"Okay, then."

But before he can turn back to the movie, I push up and lick some chocolate frosting off the side of his lip.

"You had a—"

"Riley," he growls, and throws his head back on the couch. "Killing me."

"Sorry." I clear my throat and turn my attention back to the television. "So, that old guy is a Jedi?"

"Yes. That's Obi-Won Kenobi."

"I thought Ewan McGregor played him."

"He does, in the prequels."

"Oh." I nod, as if I get it, but I don't get it at all. "Why aren't we watching the prequels first?"

"Because we're watching them in the order they were released," he replies. "Trust me, it'll be great."

I nod again and watch for a long while in silence, taking bites of cupcakes and leaning my head on Trevor's shoulder.

I have no idea what is happening in the movie.

And I don't even care. All I know is, Trevor's hard body is pressed against mine, and he's warm and strong and my libido is in overdrive.

Jesus, I understand that he wants to take things kind of slow because we're not just a fling, but how long is a girl supposed to wait before the guy she's hot after attacks her?

And why am I waiting for him to make the first move? We're living in the twenty-first century, for fuck sake.

"God, I love this part," he says, his eyes pinned to the

screen. The fist not holding on to my hip is fisted, and he's just all tensed up, and I can't stand it anymore.

I want him.

Now.

So I straddle him, grab his face in my hands, and kiss the fuck out of him. When I pull away, he's smiling up at me, his hands firmly planted on my ass.

"What's that for?"

"I want you to show me your lightsaber," I reply, and bite his lower lip. "Right now."

"I had no idea that *Star Wars* would have this effect on you."

"I know, who knew?" I settle against him more firmly, my core rubbing against his already hard cock through his basketball shorts.

They don't leave *anything* to the imagination.

And rather than push me away, his grip on my ass tightens and he pulls me against him.

"Do you just hate it and this is your way to distracting me?"

"No." I shove my fingers through his hair and smile. "I don't hate it. But I *do* want you, and if it's all the same to you, I'd rather not wait anymore."

"I don't want to push you too fast," he says as his hands roam up and down my back, my sides, and over my ass. His hands are just *everywhere,* and dear, sweet baby Jesus, they're amazing.

"Trust me when I say, this is not too fast for me."

"You're sure?"

"I'm not going to beg for it," I reply, and sit back just a bit so I can see his face. I take a deep breath, trying to clear my underfucked head so I can try to read his face. "If *you're* not ready, just say so."

He doesn't answer me; instead a slow smile spreads over his ridiculously handsome face and his hands gentle as he drags them over my sides to my chest.

He cups a breast in each hand, over my shirt, and continues to watch my face as X-wing Starfighters zip around on the TV behind me.

"I'm going to mute that," he finally says as he reaches for the remote and cuts the sound. "I'd rather hear you."

"I don't usually make much noise."

"No?"

I shake my head and bite my lip, suddenly a bit shy. Not that I want to stop, because I definitely *don't*. But now that it's here, I'm not sure what to do.

I hope he knows what he's doing, or else we're in for a night full of embarrassing moments.

"You've also never had sex with me," he says softly.

"True."

"So we don't know if you'll make a lot of noise when I'm inside you."

Fucking hell.

My pussy shivers, thighs tense.

"You like it when I talk dirty, Riley?"

I nod and close my eyes when he glides the pad of his thumbs over my nipples, still over the shirt.

I need to get rid of these clothes.

We both need to strip.

But I can't bring myself to move quite yet.

"What else do you like?"

"Everything you're doing right now is fantastic," I reply, and sigh when he lifts his hips, rubbing himself against me.

"If I do something you don't like, just say so, okay?"

"I can do that."

"Good girl."

And suddenly he stands up, carrying me to the bedroom.

"You're strong. I'm not a tiny girl."

"You like to be carried." He says it as if that explains everything, and when we reach his bed, he lowers me to stand on the floor. "I need you to stand right here for a few minutes, okay?"

I nod and watch as he takes two steps back, his eyes pinned to my body, and he strips out of his T-shirt, reaching over his head and gripping it in that sexy way men do, whipping it off in one swift motion.

The next thing I know, he's dropped his shorts as well, and he's standing before me in only what God gave him.

And, I have to tell you, God was generous.

My knees feel weak and he isn't even touching me.

He slowly steps back to me and kisses my forehead. His fingers tangle in my hair for a moment before he tugs the hem of my plain black shirt over my head and tosses it on the floor next to his things. His eyes are roaming all over me, and I have to say, he's fantastic for my ego. The man is devouring me with his eyes.

I don't know if I've ever had as intimate a moment with anyone else in my life.

His nimble fingers make quick work of my pants and underwear, and I'm standing naked before this sexy man.

I take a step back to the bed, but he shakes his head slowly back and forth.

"I said stay where you are."

I cock a brow. "Bossy."

"Oh yeah." He smiles as he leans in to kiss my neck. "I'm bossy in the bedroom, sweetheart."

"Oh, good."

I feel him grin against my collarbone. "I'm going to enjoy every square inch of your beautiful body tonight."

"Oh, good," I repeat, and plunge my hands in his hair as he nibbles his way down to my breasts. My knees want to give.

"Don't sit down," he warns me. His voice is as gentle as the fingers brushing over my sides. "I will tell you when you can move."

Do I like men this controlling when it comes to sex?

I wouldn't know. No one I've ever been with has been this bossy. In fact, they've mostly been too cautious, waiting for me to make moves.

This is a whole new ball game.

And I like it. A lot.

Trevor squats in front of me, kisses down my stomach, around my navel, and down my pubis.

Thank God I got waxed last week.

"This is beautiful," he whispers, and plants a wet kiss on

my sensitive skin, just above my clit, then blows gently, giving me goose bumps. "I love how responsive you are."

I can't even talk. All I can do is focus all my energy on staying upright because my legs want to give out.

But I want to please him.

I guess I'll have to hand in my feminist card.

His fingers trail down to my clit, barely brushing over it, and then sink into my lips. I brace myself on his strong shoulders, unable to keep my eyes open any longer.

I feel drunk on him.

"Fucking hell you're wet."

I nod in agreement because that's all I *can* do.

"Does this feel good?"

I nod again.

"Are your knees feeling weak?"

"They always feel weak when I'm with you," I reply honestly.

He doesn't say anything for a long moment, so I open my eyes to find him gazing up at me with fire in his green eyes. His fingers are still working magic in my core.

I'm no virgin, but I've never felt anything like *this*.

"Sit on the bed."

I oblige him, and in one swift motion, he urges me onto my back, covering me with his body. He kisses down my torso again, harder this time, biting and sucking. When he gets to my pussy, he doesn't hesitate, he just sinks right in, licking and kissing, massaging my ass cheeks as he lifts me up to his mouth so he can devour me.

Holy. Fucking. Shit.

My hips won't stop circling, following his tongue, begging for more. I'm gripping on to the blanket, every nerve ending in my body is zinging in pleasure.

He sinks two fingers inside me, and that's it, I come apart, crying out his name as I come harder than I ever have before. He doesn't let up as wave after wave takes me under and I'm left panting and sweating, moaning.

Is that *my* voice?

Before I have time to overthink anything, my legs are pushed up, knees to my shoulders, and he's plunging inside me, watching me.

"You're so fucking sexy."

I grab his ass, pulling him, urging him to fuck me harder.

"You like it harder?"

I nod.

"I can't go softly this time, Riley." He's breathing so hard, his pulse pounding in his neck. He lets my legs down so I can wrap them around his waist and he can cradle my head in his hands as he kisses me and fucks me.

I can't help but clench around him with each thrust, and just as I feel the next orgasm push its way down my spine, he growls and grinds his pubic bone against me, coming hard.

Did that just happen?

Oh yeah. It happened.

He kisses my cheek, my neck, my forehead, and then slides to the side of me, taking his weight off me.

"My God." He tugs me into his arms and hugs me tightly.

"I'm sorry that was so fast. I've wanted you for what feels like years, and I just couldn't hold back."

"There was nothing wrong with what we just did," I reply, and brush a lock of his hair off his forehead. "I guess now I know what all the fuss is about."

He smiles, but wrinkles his nose. "You're no virgin."

"No, but this was . . . New."

Suddenly he sits up, pinning me in a shocked expression. "What's wrong?"

"I didn't use a condom. Oh my God, Riley, I'm so sorry."

"It's okay." I wave him off and scratch my belly. "I've got that covered. Although I am assuming you're healthy—"

"Perfectly healthy."

"Me too." I smile and rub his arm. "We're good."

"Thank God. I've never forgotten protection before." He gazes at me as he lies next to me. "So now we *both* know what all the fuss is about."

"I guess we do." I want to ask him so many questions that I probably *don't* want to know the answers to. So I keep quiet and just enjoy this moment, snuggled up with him after some pretty impressive sex, and will myself not to overthink this.

Just be happy, Riley.

"Good morning," Trevor says with a sleepy voice from behind me. He's spooning me.

"Good morning." I crack an eye open. "Is it light out yet?"

"No, it's only six thirty." He pats my hip gently. "I just wake up early."

"I do too," I reply with a yawn, and lean back against him. My body is well sexed; muscles I forgot I had are already singing, and I haven't even left the bed yet.

Of course, four rounds of energetic sex in one night will do that to a girl.

"Are you too sore?" he asks, as if he can read my mind.

"It feels good." I smile back at him. "Kind of like being sore after the gym. You worked hard for that sore."

"True." He kisses my bare shoulder. "What time did you plan to go to work today?"

"Around nine," I reply with a sigh. "I should get up soon and go home so I can get ready."

"Give me just a few more minutes," he says, holding on to me more tightly. We don't say much, we just lie here, wrapped up in each other. It feels so good to be *held*. Touched.

Maybe it feels too good, but I'm going to keep following my advice from last night and not dwell or overthink.

"If you'll give me fifteen minutes to get my shit together," he says, "I'll come with you."

"You don't have to do that."

"I'd really like to spend as much time with you this morning as I can."

I glance back again. His face is relaxed, his eyes happy, and I can't bring myself to say no.

Because the truth is, I'm not ready to say good-bye either. I have it bad.

"I'd like for you to come with me."

"Excellent." He kisses my shoulder once more and then leaves the bed. I pull the sheet around me, enjoying the warmth from him against my naked body while he gets some things together and dresses. It doesn't take him long, so I finally get up and pull my clothes from yesterday back on.

The drive to my house is quiet. It's not an uncomfortable silence, just two people still trying to wake up feeling comfortable in the other's company.

It's easier than I've ever known.

THE SHOWER FELT like heaven. What is it with everything in the world feeling better after you've had some pretty impressive sex?

I don't know, but I want to keep doing it.

I've just dried off and am hanging up my wet towel when Trevor comes through the bathroom door carrying a cup from Starbucks.

"You need this." His eyes are pinned to mine as he hands me my drink.

"I'm going to take you up on the running-off-with-you thing," I reply, and sip my drink, closing my eyes in happiness as the caffeine immediately hits my bloodstream. "How did you know this was my drink?"

"I've brought you coffee at work every morning since I've been here," he reminds me. "Drink more of that."

I'm not even self-conscious standing here naked, sipping my coffee. He's looking me up and down now, his green eyes shining in approval. The way he freaking worshiped my body last night tells me that he has zero issues with any curves I may have.

Or may not have.

Because while my hips are curvy, I'm lacking in the boob department.

"What are you thinking?" he asks.

"That I could probably use a boob job," I reply with a laugh.

"No way," he replies. and leans in to nuzzle my neck. "You're perfect just as you are."

"And you're sweet." I kiss his cheek. "I need to get dressed."

"Hmm." His strong hand glides down my naked back to my ass. He pats it as he pulls away. "Okay. I also brought breakfast."

"You're pretty great, you know."

He turns back and offers me a smug smile. "I know."

Whoever was stupid enough to cheat on this man and let him go is an absolute moron.

And I'm so thankful she was.

Because I don't plan to take even one minute of any of this for granted.

I quickly dress, twist my hair into a bun, and put on my makeup. My cup is almost empty when I walk into the living room and see Trevor in my favorite chair, bundled up in a fluffy throw blanket.

"Chilly?" I ask as he holds his hand out for me. I take it and he tugs me into his lap, wrapping me in the cocoon.

"My rental doesn't have any throws like this. Which makes sense, they'd have to wash them after every time it's rented. But I get cold sitting in the living room."

"I did notice it was a bit chilly last night." I grin when he holds a bite of coffee cake to my lips. "Of course, we heated things up fast enough."

"Sex is absolutely better than a throw blanket," he agrees, and takes a bite of his own cake. "How are you this morning, now that you've had a chance to wake up?"

"I'm fantastic," I reply honestly. "The hot shower loosened up my muscles, and I just feel like I had a great time last night."

"I'm glad." He kisses my forehead and offers me another bite of cake. "This feels good too."

"Mmm." I bury my face in his neck and take a deep breath. He feels good. I can't help but wonder if this is too good to be true. Is there going to be another shoe to drop?

I mean, maybe he's been to jail. Or there's a warrant out for his arrest. Or he likes green beans.

I smirk and kiss his warm skin.

I need to stop being so cynical and believe that there really *are* nice men out there, and I finally found one.

Please don't break my heart.

His arms tighten around me in a hug.

"We should go," he whispers.

"I know." But I don't move. I just stay here, in his arms, soaking him in. Just for one more moment.

Chapter Eight

~Trevor~

$\mathcal{J}$ just sniped him," I say into my headset, and take a sip of my water. It's the first Wednesday of the month, which means it's group night. I get together with five other gamers to play and talk.

I've been playing with this same group for close to fifteen years, through two different game systems. We're friends, and we don't bring others into our fold, unless it's one of their children who wants to play for a bit.

"Let's take a break, guys," Angie says. "I need to hit the bathroom and grab a snack."

"Good timing," Scott says. I set my controller in my lap and lean back, taking another sip of my beer. "How are you feeling, Smitty?"

"Good as new," Smitty replies. That's not his *real* name, it's his gamer name. And he had a heart attack last year, which sent us all into a tailspin. "My wife has me on a strict diabetic diet, so I don't enjoy food enough to actually eat it anymore."

"Good," I reply with a laugh. "We don't need a repeat of last year."

"Agreed," Spade, another alias name, says. "My wife's dad had a heart attack last month. I feel like everyone's dropping like flies."

"I'm not dropping," Smitty says.

"I'm back, guys," Angie says, her voice breathy from rushing. "Sorry, what did I miss?"

"Smitty feels good," I reply.

"Good," Angie replies.

"Hey, Trev, how's Riley?" Scott asks.

"She's great."

"Wait, who's Riley?" Angie asks.

"She's a woman I've been seeing," I reply as the game starts again.

"I haven't heard you talk about her before."

"It's pretty new," I reply with a scowl. "And I don't tell you guys *everything*."

"Really?" Scott asks, with sarcasm dripping through the line. "Good because I don't want to know everything."

"I do," Angie says. She sounds pretty pissed off, which makes me raise a brow. "Where the hell did you meet her?"

"In Portland," I reply shortly.

"You're in *Portland*? Or did you meet her online?"

"Hey, why the hostility?" Trent, the sixth in our group, asks. He's the quietest of all of us.

"I'm not hostile." Angie sniffs. "I just want the scoop."

"I'm in Portland working on a show," I reply, not that I have to explain myself to Angie or anyone else. "She's one of the co-owners of the restaurant I'm working in."

"Oh."

"You okay, Ange?" Scott asks. A text from Scott comes through my phone. We often text back and forth, privately discussing what's happening in the group.

What's up with her?

I shrug, as if he can see me, and reply. No idea.

"Fine." We're all quiet for a moment as we run around and shoot the enemy. Finally, Angie says, "You know what? I have to go. I forgot about something I have to do."

"Angie, you can't leave in the middle of a game," Scott says, but before he can finish, she's gone.

"Now we're down a man," Spade says.

"It's okay, we've got this," I mutter, and the five of us concentrate on picking up Angie's slack. When the round is over, we lose, but only by a tiny bit. "We'll get them on the next round."

"I wonder what was up Angie's ass?" Smitty says.

"You know how possessive she can be," Trent says. "She doesn't like new women coming into our group. She acted this way every time one of us met our wives."

"True," Scott says. "Maybe it's a chick thing."

"And being the only girl in our group for so long," I add. "I thought she had a boyfriend?"

"Angie changes boyfriends with the seasons," Smitty says. He's the closest to her. "I think they broke it off a couple of weeks ago."

"You don't think she has a thing for Trevor, do you?" Scott says, and I immediately laugh.

"No way," I reply.

"That would be like his sister having a thing for him," Spade says. "Weird."

"I don't know," Scott continues. "She sounded pretty jealous. And you guys know as well as I do that Angie likes the gamer dudes. The only reason she hasn't tried to get with any of us is because we're all happily married. But Trevor's not married."

"If what you say is true," Trent says, "hearing that he's met someone new would have made her pretty mad. She's always been the dramatic type."

"Trust me, guys, Angie doesn't have a thing for me," I say, and laugh. "She's probably just having a shitty day."

Suddenly there's a knock at my door.

"Don't start the new game yet, someone's at my door."

"Trevor's so getting laid tonight," Scott says.

"Shut it," I mutter, and pull the door open to find a very sexy Riley waiting behind it. "Hi, sweetheart."

"I know, it's game night, and I'm not staying," she says in a rush as she walks past me into the kitchen. "I just had to bring you a few things."

"I can sign off."

"Hey, bros before hoes, remember?" Smitty asks, making the others laugh.

"Are they in your ear now?" Riley asks with a smile.

"Oh yeah."

"Hi, guys!" she calls out, aiming at the mouthpiece. "I'm not staying!"

She begins unloading a big plastic bag.

"I just wanted to make sure you're well fed," she says, making me smile. She's in her old college sweatshirt and a pair of jeans that do awesome things for her ass.

I'm such an ass man.

"And I needed to make sure you're warm."

The last thing she pulls out of her bag is a black throw blanket, very much like the one I curled up with the other day at her house. She flicks it open, and reveals the Death Star.

"It's *Star Wars*," she says proudly.

"Yes, it is," I reply, and pull my earbud out of my ear so I can kiss my girl without an audience. I grip her waist and pull her to me. "Thank you, Riley."

"You're welcome," she says, and melts into me, her hands on my chest. "I really didn't want to interrupt your evening. I know this is your night with the guys."

"I can take a minute to kiss you," I reply, and lower my lips to hers, brushing them lightly and then settling in to taste her, to make her go just a little weak in the knees. "Stay," I whisper.

"I can't," she whispers back, and grins against my mouth. "Tonight is DVR night with Cami. I have a date with a vampire."

"Convenient," I reply, and brush my fingertips down her

cheek, unable to keep from touching her. "Thank you, for all of this. You didn't have to."

"I know." She kisses me once more and then pulls away, walking toward the door. "Enjoy it all and I'll see you tomorrow. You hear that, guys? He's all mine tomorrow! I'm not sharing."

I plug the bud back in my ear in time to hear the guys laughing.

"Be safe tonight."

"Always." She blows me a kiss and then she's gone.

"What did she bring you?" Scott asks.

"Looks like a salad from the restaurant, some brownies, and a *Star Wars* blanket because this rental doesn't have any throws."

"Aw, she got you a blankie," Smitty says, making us all laugh.

She did. She pays attention. It might be the sweetest thing anyone's ever done for me.

Ever.

I don't know if that's sad, or if she's just really great. I'm going with she's great.

"It was nice of her," I say, and sit on the couch, the blanket over my lap and my food spread around me. "I have supplies, so I'm ready to go back in when you guys are."

"We were just waiting for you to be lovesick," Trent says. "But in all seriousness, she sounds like a nice girl. I'm happy for you."

"Thanks, man."

"Okay, let's go kill some zombies," Scott says, and we

jump into the next game and play late into the night. Tomorrow morning will come early, but I wouldn't give these evenings up for anyone. Well, I would for Riley if she needed me, but I hope she continues to understand that although this hobby of mine is totally geeky, it's important to me.

Time will tell.

My ex didn't get it. It's one of the many reasons that our relationship just didn't work out.

But Riley is different from anyone I've been with in the past. Not only is she sweet and beautiful, but she's not completely self-absorbed. She thinks of others first.

And that just makes me want to give to and protect her fiercely.

"Earth to Trevor," Scott says in my ear. "Are you going to shoot these fucking zombies or are you going moon over Riley all night?"

"Fuck off," I mumble, and focus on the game at hand. "I shoot double the zombies you do."

"Prove it."

"She's nervous," Riley whispers in my ear the next morning. We're just about to wrap a shoot of Mia cooking with our host in the kitchen. She's smiling, but forgets to look up at the camera.

"She's doing great," I reply softly.

"I know that, and *you* know that, but Mia is self-conscious," Riley replies, watching her friend. "She always has been."

"I'll talk to her," I reply, and pat Riley on the back. We've been careful to keep our relationship on the down-low at the restaurant. Not that everyone doesn't already know that we're seeing each other when we're not here, but there's no reason to act like lovesick teenagers.

I'm capable of keeping my hands to myself.

Sort of.

"Thanks," Riley says, and smiles up at me. "I have a meeting, so I'll be in my office if you need anything."

"Sounds good. Oh, before I forget, would you like to go to Multnomah Falls with me on Saturday? I've always heard that it's beautiful there, and thought I'd check it out."

She bites her lip. "I would love to, but I'm supposed to go hang out with my nana on Saturday. I can reschedule—"

"Definitely not," I reply, and kiss her cheek. "I didn't know you were close with your nana."

She nods. "She's my dad's mother, and we grew very close after he passed away. She's actually a lot of fun."

"Good." I nod as my cameraman waves at me, signaling that we're almost finished. "Enjoy her, and we can see the falls another day."

"Sunday?"

"Perfect."

She nods and rushes into her office as I walk toward Mia, staying just out of the camera's view.

"And that's it," she says with a shrug. "Wait. Let me do that again."

She takes a deep breath, then looks up at the camera and smiles widely. "And that's it. Trust me, if you follow this recipe, your guests will never want to leave your house."

"And, cut," the director says with a happy nod. "We've got it."

Mia sighs in relief as the crew shuts down the lights and begins to clear out of the kitchen. We're done shooting for today.

I join Mia and pat her shoulder. "You did great."

"Really?" She wrinkles her nose. "I'm trying to get better about looking at the camera rather than down at the food all the time. I've never had to concentrate on anything other than the food before."

"I get it, but you're really a natural," I reply with a nod. "In fact, I've been thinking about talking to you about doing the *Chef vs. Chef* show we do. Have you seen it?"

"Of course," she says. "But you can't seriously want me to go head-to-head with a celebrity chef."

"Why not? Mia, after this hour-long special about your restaurant airs, *you'll* be a celebrity chef."

She rolls her eyes. "No, I won't. I'll just be that girl who was on TV once."

"Not if I have anything to say about it," I reply with a grin. "You are beautiful, the camera loves you, and you know exactly what you're doing in the kitchen. Viewers would devour it."

"Trevor, I think you're really sweet to say all of those things, but look at me." She holds her arms out to the side and looks down herself. "I'm not exactly the usual body type for television. I'm way too heavy for that."

"You're wrong," I reply, and hold my hand up when she frowns and looks like she's going to argue with me. "Hear me out, Mia. Your curves are beautiful, first of all. Your hair is ridiculously pretty, and I know it's not usual to wear your hair down in the kitchen, but they probably would have you do exactly that when filming the show."

"That's not sanitary," she says with a frown.

"It's for TV, not for serving a wedding party," I reply. "Plus, and you may not believe this, but you *are* very pretty. Many chefs are curvy, and are still on TV. Trisha Yearwood, Ina Garten, Rachael Ray. That's the beauty of television about food, the stars are all shapes and sizes, all ages. You're awesome, Mia. Trust me, this is what I do for a living."

"I'll give it some thought," she murmurs softly. "I don't love having you in my kitchen, I'm not going to lie about that. But if it was just one episode . . ."

"We could start with one," I reply, and smile when her head whips up to mine.

"Trevor, I don't want Good Bites TV parked in my kitchen indefinitely."

"I get it." I hold my hands up in surrender. "Let's get this special under our belts first, and see what happens."

"Okay." She sighs. "How much longer do we have of filming?"

"I'd like to do another round of interviews with each of you, and then a full day of interviewing you as a group."

"How long is this special?" she asks with a scowl. "We've already given you hours of footage."

"And it'll all get scrutinized and cut down to an hour," I reply with a smile. "That's not my department. I just have to make sure we have plenty of footage for the editors."

"Okay," she says. "You're the expert."

"That I am."

"You're also very cozy with Riley."

It's amazing to watch the switch flip instantly from chef to best friend.

"That's also true."

"You're good for her," she says as she wipes down a countertop with a white rag. She tosses it into a nearby sink and leans her hips against the counter, her arms crossed, and looks me in the eyes. "Are you going to hurt her?"

"No, ma'am, that's not my goal in the least."

"It doesn't have to be your goal for it to happen," she says. "I mean, only a *monster* gets with a woman with the intention of mind-fucking her later."

"True."

"Riley's a good person. She's probably the best of all of us. She's not innocent, or even naive really, but she's *good,* you know?"

"I do. I was just thinking the same last night."

She nods. "She's met some real douchebags. Then again, most of us have."

"And it's not just men who have the market on douche-baggery," I remind her. "I've met my share."

"Oh, for sure," she says with a nod. "If I'm being honest, I can be a douchebag."

"I think you're just a master at defending your heart," I reply, and she blinks rapidly.

"You hardly know me."

"I know." I shrug. "I'm a people watcher, and I overthink most things. I'm sorry if that made you uncomfortable."

"It's okay." She watches me for a moment. "Let me tell you something about Riley, Trevor. She'll expect you to disappear. Most of the men in her life haven't stuck around. They die, or they bail. So this whole long-distance thing makes me nervous."

"It doesn't excite me either," I reply with a sigh, and push my hand through my hair. "But I've already told her, this isn't a fling for me. Neither of us wants that."

"Good." She smiles. "As long as you're on the same page, that's all a person can do."

"I would say that we are, indeed, on the same page."

"Maybe that's why you'd like to force me to do more shows for you, so you have a reason to spend a large amount of time in Portland."

"I already have a reason for that," I remind her. "I don't have to make excuses to be with Riley. If that's what we both want, I'll make it happen whether there's a show involved or not. If need be, I can work in television locally."

"That must be a step down, to go from national to local television."

"The money is the same," I reply with a shrug, and then scowl. "But we're not talking about me."

"No?" She grins, a smug Cheshire cat smile, and then chuckles. "I think you've given me all the answers I need."

"You're a good friend," I say.

"Oh yeah." She nods slowly. "There are two things in this

life that I'm fucking excellent at, and it's cooking and being there for my friends. Those are the two constants in my life that I can depend on no matter what, so I'm not going to fuck either of them up."

"Good for you," I reply, thinking of my group of friends spread all over the country, and our Wednesday-night games. "And I totally understand."

"Good." She wipes her hands on a towel. "Now that we understand each other, get out of my kitchen. I have to prepare for dinner."

"Yes, ma'am." I grin and turn to stroll out, wondering what Riley's up to, when Mia calls me back.

"Trevor."

"Yeah." I glance back over my shoulder.

"It goes without saying that if you hurt her, I'll kill you and make it look like an accident."

If it were anyone else, I'd smirk, but Mia isn't playing.

"I know."

"Okay, then."

Chapter Nine

~Riley~

*A*nd then I said, you listen here, Douglass Smooter, I don't care if you were the king of England, you will *not* tell me who I can vote for in this election."

Nana is on a roll. I sit back in her dining room chair, holding my tea in both hands, and smile at her. "And what did he say?"

"Oh, he just went on about how he used to be the mayor of some small town in Washington, and he knows how government is supposed to be run, blah blah blah." She rolls her blue eyes and reaches up to fluff her salt-and-pepper hair.

"What were you voting on?"

"Why, the president of the domino club, of course."

I hide my smile behind my teacup. "Of course. Who won?"

"I did."

"Good for you." She reaches her fist out for a bump, and I oblige her. My nana is the coolest woman I know. Self-confident, funny, and smart as hell, she gives everyone in her retirement community a run for their money. "How is Mr. Lewis?"

"Who, dear?"

"Mr. Lewis. The guy you were dating last month."

"Oh." She waves that off and fills her cup with more tea. "He was entirely too old for me."

"You said he was sixty-eight."

"Exactly."

"You're seventy-two."

"Yes, and I've decided to spend my time on the younger men. No one older than sixty-five, Riley. These old geezers can't keep up with me. I need them to be younger, with more energy."

"Why not just go for a guy in his forties?"

"Don't think I haven't," she says with a wink, and I immediately scowl.

"Ew. I don't think I really want to know this."

"Oh, stop it. We're both grown adults." She waves me off and takes a sip, watching me with those shrewd blue eyes that look so much like mine. "Having gentlemen callers keeps us young."

"Sure." I roll my eyes, not wanting to give even one thought to what my grandmother does with these gentlemen callers. Surely, she doesn't sleep with them.

Right?

Because, that's just disturbing.

"Please tell me you've met a nice young man. It's time you do. You can't pine away after that guy, oh, what was his name? Rick? Ralf?"

"Logan," I reply with a laugh. "And I'm not pining away after him. But I'd been with him for a whole year, Nana, and he left with no explanation. I think I was entitled to be pretty hurt over that."

"I agree, but you need to meet someone new."

"Actually, I have," I reply, and try to act all nonchalant about it, but Nana's eyes widen and she smiles widely.

"Finally! Tell me *everything*. How's the sex?"

"Nana!"

"Oh, for Pete's sake, Riley Marie, you're an adult woman with needs. Please tell me you're not doing something stupid like holding out for marriage."

"You know, most parents actually *do* advise their children to hold out for marriage."

"I'm your nana, not your mother, not that she held out for marriage either. I'm quite sure she was no virgin when she and my son met."

"I can't even believe I'm having this conversation with you," I mutter, and press my fingertips to my eyes, praying for the floor to open up and swallow me.

"Oh, we're having it. And if it makes you feel any better, I have my share of sex too."

"No. No, it doesn't make me feel any better."

She laughs with delight and slaps her hand on the table.

"Hey, at least I can't get pregnant these days. Makes the whole birth-control thing easier."

I can't help but laugh with her now. "Nana, you are absolutely one of a kind."

"Of course I am. And so are you." She pats my hand. "So keep the sex to yourself if you must, but tell me about him."

"He's actually the main producer for the TV show we're filming at the restaurant this month." I take a sip of tea and try to form the best description of him in my mind. "He's tall, I'd say about six-foot-two."

"I was always a fan of a tall gentleman caller myself," she says with a knowing nod.

"I love that you call them gentleman callers."

"Well, they are, darling." She grins. "Keep going."

"Right. So, he's tall, and he has light brown hair with green eyes, and he wears these dark, thick-rimmed glasses that are so freaking hot."

"Mm-hmm," she says with a nod. "Glasses are definitely sexy."

My nana just said "sexy."

"He has great hands," I continue. "And he's intelligent. He likes video games, but he works out too."

"So he has a nice balance in his life," Nana says.

"I think so," I reply with a nod. "He's no couch potato."

"No, you wouldn't be attracted to that," she says. "And you said he works for the television company?"

"The network, yes."

"Where does he live?"

"Los Angeles," I reply with a wince, and stand to boil

more water in the kettle on her stovetop. Her refrigerator is covered with monthly calendars, each day filled in with reminders for tai chi, domino nights, bowling, bingo, yoga, and swim aerobics.

The woman never stops moving, and I'm pretty sure that's what is going to keep her alive to about one hundred years old.

"Do you enjoy the tai chi?" I ask.

"Oh yes, it's very relaxing and good for the circulation. You should come for it."

I smile at the thought of doing tai chi with a big group of seniors. It actually sounds like fun, but I can't make it up here at the time of their class.

"And don't change the subject," she says. "How are you going to pursue something with this man if he lives in Southern California? And what is his name, anyway?"

"Trevor," I reply, and fill both of our cups. "He's in his midthirties, so he's older than me."

"Nothing wrong with that," Nana says thoughtfully.

"You're going after the young ones," I remind her, but she just laughs and shakes her head.

"That's for *me*. We're talking about you now. Do you have a photo of him? Do you take selfies?"

"Do *you* take selfies?" I ask her as I wake my phone up and find the few selfies we've taken together. We don't do it often.

"Of course I do, Riley. This is 2017."

"Of course." I show her a photo of Trevor and me and watch as Nana's face softens.

"Oh, you make a handsome couple."

"Thank you."

"I don't want you to move to Southern California."

"I'm not." I tuck my phone back in my handbag. "My business is here, you're here, my friends, my life, everything is here. I don't plan to and don't want to move to L.A."

"Is he going to move here, then?"

I frown. "I don't think so. His job is down there. Besides, it's still pretty new. We haven't really talked about this stuff."

"When does he leave?"

"He has about a week and a half left in filming," I reply, and feel an instant heaviness in my shoulders. I don't want to think about him leaving already.

"Well, I think you'll figure it out together," Nana says with a reassuring smile. "If it's meant to be, it'll be just fine."

"Right." I nod and change the subject. "Are you going down to play dominoes tonight?"

"Of course, darling, I'm the president," she says with a toothy smile. When I was a kid, she'd take out her teeth and make me laugh. Thankfully, she keeps them in these days. "You should come with me."

"Oh, I can't stay all evening."

"It starts at four o'clock," she says.

"That's in half an hour."

"Yes, so you should just stay and go with me."

"Okay." I frown. "Why is it so early in the day? It says on your calendar that it's 'Domino Night.'"

"Riley, four o'clock *is* nighttime for many of the people

here, the old geezers. If they're not in bed by seven, they think the sky is going to fall."

I stifle a laugh. "I'm sure it's not that bad."

"You'll see for yourself." She rolls her eyes, as if she just can't believe that the others would want to go to bed so early. Nana has always been so young at heart. She never wants to stop learning and doing, and I love that about her.

We clean our tea mess, and gather our things to go down to the community room, where the tables and chairs are already set up. Each table has four chairs, and a box of dominoes sitting in the middle. In the rear of the room is a long table set up with some snacks and drinks.

"You go all out," I comment, and follow her to the heart of the room, where she sets down her things and nods as she looks around.

"They did a good job of setting up," Nana replies. "If you would like to play, I can kick someone out of our table."

"No." I shake my head. "I'll grab a snack and a drink and pull up a chair and watch you and your friends."

"Are you sure?"

"Of course."

People have started to filter in, claiming their seats and gathering refreshments, and before I know it, the room is full of laughter, chatter, and some pretty enthusiastic domino playing.

Of course, Nana has three men with her at her table.

"So, beauty runs in the family," the man to my right says. I've already forgotten their names. All I see is one man with the bushiest eyebrows in the history of eyebrows, one with a handlebar mustache, and one with a ponytail. It's Mr. Ponytail who's commenting on our gene pool.

"Nana was always beautiful," I reply with a smile just as my phone rings. "Hi, Trevor."

Nana smiles, her eyes lighting up like it's Christmas morning.

"Hello, beautiful. How did your visit with your nana go?"

"Great. In fact, it's still going."

"Oh, I'm sorry to interrupt," he says, and before he can say good-bye, Nana taps me on the arm.

"Have him come join us," she says with an encouraging nod.

"Was that her?" he asks.

"That's her. Do you want to come play some dominoes?" I bite my lip, fully expecting him to say no thanks, but he shocks the hell out of me.

"Absolutely. Where am I going?"

I relay the address, name of the retirement community, and give him directions, then hang up.

"He'll be here in about thirty minutes."

"Well, I'll miss him," Mr. Handlebar Mustache says. "It's getting pretty late for me."

I glance down at my phone, see that it's just shy of six o'clock, and share a smile with Nana.

"Me too," Mr. Colossal Eyebrows says.

"Well, that means that you and your gentleman caller can play with Pete and me," Nana says with a wink.

And I was mistaken. Trevor comes sauntering in just

fifteen minutes later, looking sexier than fuck in a leather jacket, his jeans, and those hot glasses.

"Hello," Nana whispers, then stands to shake Trevor's hand. "I'm Riley's nana, Dolores."

"I don't believe that," Trevor replies with a charming smile. "You have to be her mother."

"That charm will get you everywhere," she replies, and motions for him to join us. Before he does, he leans in to kiss my cheek.

"Hi," he whispers in my ear, sending the butterflies in my stomach into a tizzy.

"Welcome," I reply. "This is Pete."

The men shake hands and we begin to play. I haven't played this game since I was a kid, so it takes me a little while to remember all of the rules.

By the end of the first game, Trevor has killed us all.

"He's a domino shark," Nana says with a wink. "If I was forty years younger, I'd give Riley a run for her money with you, Trevor."

"Don't tease me now, Miss Dolores," Trevor replies with a grin. "I have a feeling I'd fall right in love with you."

"Of course you would." Her smile is smug and her blue eyes are shining in happiness. Watching the man I'm interested in flirt with my nana is just . . . *funny*.

Trevor's phone is sitting between him and me, and it suddenly lights up with a notification of a Facebook message from someone named Angie.

He glances down at it, frowns, then flips the phone over, facedown, and continues playing dominoes.

"You're not going to check that?" I ask him.

"No, she's just a gamer friend. It's nothing important." He kisses my cheek and resumes talking with Pete, and my butterflies have all decided to sleep. I'm not typically a jealous woman. But I had no idea that he gamed with women. I just assumed they were all guys.

Sexist of me? Perhaps.

I don't like it.

But rather than confront him and act like a crazy person, I set it aside for tonight and enjoy the banter between Nana and Trevor, and the way he rests his hand on my thigh under the table.

"I NEED YOUR advice," I say to Addie the next day. We're in our office, and we're the first to arrive today. Trevor stayed with me last night, but he had a phone conference this morning, so we took our own cars to work.

Which is fine with me because I need to pick Addie's brain.

"Yes, you should have sex with Trevor," she replies, and rolls her eyes. "I mean, get it on already."

"We're already doing that," I reply. "But something weird happened last night."

I tell her about Trevor receiving the message from Angie and his response to it.

"What would you do if it was Jake?"

"I'd demand to know who the fuck Angie is," Addie says. "But we're married, and I already know all of his friends."

"I'm being serious."

"So am I." She sits back in her chair and taps her pen against her lips, her eyes narrowed in thought. "He's never mentioned her before?"

"No, but he never said there *weren't* women who he gamed with either."

"Is it weird that I'm surprised that there are women who play video games as intently as men?"

"No, I thought it was unusual too, and then I felt like a sexist."

"Me too," she says with a laugh. "Okay. The important thing is, you don't have any reason to not trust Trevor. Right?"

"True. I mean, he spends most of his time with me. But I'm seriously worried that there might be another shoe to drop at some point. I mean, he's *amazing* with a capital *A*. That can't be normal."

"Jake is pretty great too," she says with a shrug. "There are men out there who aren't assholes. I know, it's like an elusive kind of wildcat that's only ever been seen once in the wild, but they exist."

"So I'm overreacting."

"Maybe," she replies. "But I get it. It would look suspicious to me if he brushed it off that easily. So just keep your eyes and ears open, and if something bothers you, talk to him about it. Jake's always reminding me that he's not a mind reader."

"I'm such a cynic."

"With good reason, Ri. Okay, what are some of your deal breakers, besides things like child molestation, murder, et cetera, that he could tell you and you'd run away?"

"Well, if he said he has a girlfriend back home, that would not be good."

"Do you think this Angie is his girlfriend?" she asks with a frown. "I mean, wouldn't she just text him?"

"Good point."

"Next on your list?"

"What if he has kids he hasn't told me about?"

"You're more dramatic than I am," she replies, blinking slowly. "Seriously, stop overthinking this."

"I keep telling myself the same thing! But what if—"

"Stop," she says firmly. "You can *what-if* yourself to death, Riley. What if he has a twin brother he's never met? What if he had a sixth toe on one foot when he was born and he had it removed? What if he's the heir to a fortune in Tasmania?"

"Okay, that last one was a bit of a reach, even for me."

She smirks. "Stop trying to will something bad to happen."

"That's what I'm doing, isn't it?"

"Yes, and it's not healthy. Angie is a gamer friend, and it wasn't anything important. If it was anything else, he would have said so."

"Right." I nod. "I don't know why I instantly assume he's lying to me."

"Because we've known a lot of liars," Addie says. "But I don't get that feeling about Trevor. He's good people."

"He is."

"How's the sex?" she asks, and unlike with my nana, I don't mind sharing with Addie.

"I had no idea it could feel like that," I reply. "I mean,

who knew that fireworks could *literally* go off when a girl has an orgasm?"

"Well, they don't, but it sure feels like it, right?"

"Yes! And he found my G-spot, and I have to tell you, I'm completely addicted to him."

"Good. It's about time you got laid properly."

"Boy, you're not kidding," I reply, and check my phone, but there are no messages from Trevor. "In fact, I might need to go buy some new pretty lingerie. I'd given up on all of that a few years ago."

"Oh, you absolutely need some pretty new things," she replies with a nod. "Have you waxed lately?"

"Yes, that I didn't let slide."

"Good girl. What about a pedicure?"

"It's been a while."

"I'll call Cici. We need a girls' day with her."

"Yes! Perfect. I'll get my nails done too."

"I want to go lingerie shopping with you," Addie says. "When should we go?"

I check my schedule. "Neither of us is being interviewed today."

"Spontaneous shopping trip coming up."

"Right on."

She fist-bumps me and throws her planner, some lip gloss, and phone in her handbag. "Let's go."

"Oh, you mean *right now*?"

"Hell yes, right now. I'll buy some new stuff too. I haven't done anything like that for Jake since before Ella was born."

"Awesome." I gather my things. "Let's go."

Chapter Ten

~Trevor~

That was worth the drive," I say as Riley and I pull onto the interstate headed toward Portland.

"Absolutely," she says with an enthusiastic nod. "I know that Addie and Jake come out here a lot, and now I know why. It's beautiful. I'm glad we came early in the day. There wasn't anywhere to park when we left."

"And now we have the rest of the day to do anything," I reply, and pull her hand up to my lips. Even the skin on her hands is soft. I enjoyed being with her and her nana yesterday. Seeing them together showed me a side to Riley I didn't realize was there. She's always funny, and now I know where she gets it.

Nana is a spitfire.

And someone I could see myself being friends with.

But today, I'm going to keep Riley all to myself.

Her phone buzzes and she pulls her hand out of mine to answer it.

"What the hell?" she whispers, and reads the screen. I'm driving too fast to glance over.

"Is everything okay?"

"Just a second," she says, and is quiet while she finishes reading, then lays her phone in the cup holder and turns to face me in the seat.

"What's up?" I ask.

"You tell me," she replies, and I glance over now to find her face flushed, her eyes narrowed, and her hands practically shaking with anger.

"Uh, babe, I didn't get a message on my phone. If you're going to be pissed at me, you're going to have to tell me why."

"Angie," she says. "Who the fuck is she, Trevor? Because she just sent me a pretty threatening message on Facebook, I saw her name on your phone the other night, and I need to know if I'm poaching on someone else's man."

What in the ever-loving fuck is she talking about?

I'm silent as I wait for the next exit. I pull off the interstate and into a random parking lot, throw the car out of gear, and reach for my own phone.

"Are you going to ignore me?" she demands, and I hold my hand up, stopping her.

"Give me a second," I say, my voice deceptively calm. I never bothered to read Angie's message from the other night, so I bring it up and quickly read it.

Hi Trev,

I've been doing some thinking since the other night, and I just want to tell you that no matter what happens with this Riley person, I'm here for you. I know you've had a rough few years, and I feel like I should express how much our friendship means to me. I just want you to be happy, Trevor. You so deserve it! Please call me, even if you just need to talk. Xoxo Ang

"Jesus," I mutter, and rub my fingers over my lips. "What did she say to you?"

"Does it matter?" she asks. Her arms are folded over her chest, and she's leaning away from me. Totally unacceptable.

"Yes. It matters. Please read it to me."

She rolls her eyes and reaches for her phone, finding the message.

Dear Riley,

I thought I should introduce myself to you. I'm Angie, a longtime friend of Trevor's. I understand that you've been dating him, and I wanted to just reach out and give you a heads-up about the kind of person Trevor is. I want you to be very careful when it comes to him. He's had a lot of upheaval in his life over the past few years, and this has made him very unpredictable and unbalanced. I would never want to see anyone get hurt, even someone I don't know. All of his friends, including me, are very worried about him.

Also, Trevor and I have started taking the steps to move our friendship to the next level. I am so excited! I really think he needs someone like me in his life to help him figure some things out. So I'd appreciate it if you'd kindly step aside, and let this happen for us as it's supposed to.

I'm really looking out for all parties involved.

Angie

She calmly sets the phone down, and I'm completely struck dumb.

"Well?" she asks.

"I'm so fucking shocked and angry right now," I begin, and grip on to the steering wheel like it's Angie's neck. "I need to gather my thoughts."

"Oh, good," she replies with a nod. "Well, while you're gathering your thoughts, let me tell you some of mine. Why would you pursue something with me if you've already got something going on with her?"

"I don't," I reply, and swallow hard, then turn in the seat so I can look her in the eye. "I've known Angie for about fifteen years. She's a gamer. I've met her exactly *once* in person. I don't game alone with her, ever. She's part of the group."

Riley's lips are still puckered, but she's listening, so I keep talking.

"She lives in Des Moines or Dallas or Duluth. Some *D* city." I wave that off. "Anyway, all I know is what she's told us, and who knows how much of that is true?"

"She clearly has a thing for you," Riley says, and sighs. "And frankly, I'm too old to deal with this kind of juvenile bullshit."

"If she has a thing for me, I had no clue about it, and that's the truth." I hold my hands up in surrender. "I am not lying about this. I'll talk to Angie and set her straight."

"Set her straight on which part exactly?" Riley is good and pissed now. "I mean, did you hear that? She doesn't make any fucking sense! Are you dangerous, or are you in love with her? Because she basically just said both."

"She's a fruitcake," I mutter.

"What did she say to you?" Riley asks, and I bring the message up on my phone and hand it to her. "It's so nice of her to offer to be there when I break your heart and she can pick up the pieces." She passes the phone back to me and laughs humorlessly.

"None of this was initiated by me."

"I just—" She looks out of the passenger-side window and bites her lip for a moment. "I'm so sick of men and their drama. I knew there'd be another shoe to drop."

"What does that mean?"

"Just take me home," she says, resignation in her voice. "I think I just want to be alone today."

"You know, it's ironic that *this* is the drama." I pull back onto the freeway, rage roaring through my bloodstream. I want to punch someone. I want to scream. "Even my ex-wife wouldn't stoop to this. So it's not my ex, it's not one of my sisters, it's motherfucking *Angie.*"

I shake my head and drive, frustration taking over the anger now. At Angie, me, *and* Riley, because obviously she still doesn't trust that she's the only one I'm interested in.

So I'm going to convince her.

Rather than drive her home, I take us to the apartment. Riley is staring at me as I pull into my parking space.

"Did you not hear me when I said I want to go home?"

"I heard you," I reply, turn off the car, and get out, walking over to open her door for her. "Come on."

"I'm done with you today," she says stubbornly.

"Well, I'm not done with you." I take her hand and guide her out of the car, into the building, and up to my place.

"Don't look now, but your caveman side just kicked in," she mutters.

"So be it."

I unlock the door and lead her inside, and when the door is shut, I press her up against it and cage her in.

"You're going to hear me out."

She licks her lips and watches my eyes, and I know I finally have her full attention.

"I don't give two fucks about Angie. She's not even a blip on my radar. It's *you,* Riley. You're the one I want. Jesus, I don't even see anyone else."

She frowns. "What do you mean?"

I drag my fingertips down her cheek. "You still don't get

it, do you? I'm so crazy about you I can't see straight. When you're with me, no one else exists."

I brush my lips over hers and feel her soften against me. My hand slips under her shirt and up her smooth side to cup her breast.

"Every inch of you is perfect for me." I drag my nose along her jawline to her ear. "I love the way you respond to me. Look at those goose bumps on your neck."

"I can't see my neck," she says, making me smile.

"My mistake." I pull away and lead her to the bedroom, where a full-length mirror hangs behind the door. I place her in front of it, and I come up behind and watch my hands roam over her body, still over her clothes.

Her cheeks are flushed again, but instead of anger, it's from pure lust.

"You have nothing to be jealous of," I whisper in her ear, and watch her bite her lower lip as I let my thumb press on her nipple over her bra. My cock is nestled nicely against her ass, and it's all I can do not to strip us both bare and fuck her against the mirror.

We'll get there, but not yet.

She lets her head fall back onto my shoulder.

"No, baby, I need you to watch this." She returns her gaze to mine in the mirror. Her eyelids are heavy. Her nipples are puckered.

She's fucking gorgeous.

I tug her shirt over her head and let it fall to the floor, and then unhook the front of her bra and watch as it falls open, revealing her breasts.

"You think these are too small?" I ask, my voice thick. She nods once, her eyes glued to mine. My fingers brush the tight little nipples, and then I let them rest in my hands, enjoying the light weight of them. "They're a handful for me, Riley, and I don't have small hands."

A small smile tugs at the corners of her mouth.

"Not to mention I fucking love this little freckle on the left one."

"The left one is bigger too," she whispers.

"I admit, I haven't seen every breast in the world, but I've been told that's pretty normal."

The smile spreads farther across her face, and it almost brings me to my knees.

"When you smile at me, it's like a light has been turned on in a dark room." I kiss her earlobe and continue to fondle her breasts. "I'd do anything for that smile."

"And your curves." My hands drift down to her jeans, unfasten them, and slowly lower them down her sexy legs. "I love every curve on your body."

My hands drift down her calves, to her feet and back up again.

"Your inner thighs are so fucking soft, Ri." I place wet kisses on her thighs and feel her knees shake. "You're not going to fall, are you?"

"Oh, I'm falling," she whispers, and takes a deep breath. "This is the best torture ever."

"It's not torture at all," I reply, and kiss my way over her round ass and up her spine. "I'm just telling you how amazing I think you are. Hasn't anyone ever done that before?"

She shakes her head no.

I can't stand it anymore. I scoop her up in my arms and take her to the bed, pull her panties off her, and take her in.

"Shame on every man who has had the privilege of seeing you naked." I lean in and kiss her neck again, smiling at the way her hips move in response. "You're so smart." I place a kiss on that little place where her collarbones meet. "So damn funny." Now I kiss right between her breasts. "Kindest person I know."

I lick around her navel and the piercing there. "I fucking love this piercing."

"I used to have my clitoral hood pierced," she whispers, catching my attention.

"Used to?"

She nods. "I took it out."

"Why?"

She shrugs one shoulder, like it's no big deal, but I know better. I climb back on top of her, my clothes brushing against her nakedness, and make her look me in the eye.

"Why?"

"Because a guy I dated made fun of it, so I took it off."

"Fucking asshole," I reply, instantly royally pissed off at every fucker she's been with. "He didn't deserve you."

"No." She brushes my hair out of my eyes. "He didn't."

I kiss her deeply, then continue my journey down her body. She's spread open, her pussy already wet, her clit hard and ready for me.

"I can't get enough of you." I look up at her and smile.

"That's the honest truth, Riley. I can't fucking get enough of you."

"I'm right here."

I let one finger slip down into her wet folds and watch as she tosses her head back, her eyes close, and she moans long and loud.

"This, Riley? Right here? This is mine, sweetheart."

"Oh yeah," she groans, and tilts her pelvis up for more. I circle her clit with my fingertip, then dive back down into her, spreading her delicious wetness all around.

"I can't get enough of your body." I lick her now, from anus to clit and she fists her hands in the covers at her hips. "I can't fucking get enough of making you laugh."

I reach up and tweak one nipple and she yelps.

"I never get tired of talking with you, hearing your thoughts on everything and anything."

I suck on her clit, sending her into the stratosphere, and I'm so fucking hard, my cock is pulsing against the fly of my jeans.

"I want you, Riley. I never stop wanting you. That's just it."

I free my cock and slip inside her, making us both moan in relief and pent-up lust.

"This is the most satisfying and addictive thing I've ever known. *You.*"

My hips are moving fast, pumping in and out of her. I'm full of frustration and lust. I need her to *see.* To understand.

"This is us, Riley, you and me, and no one else. No one else exists for me. Do you understand that?"

"I do now," she says breathlessly, and grips onto my hair, wrapping her legs around my waist. "I'm sorry I doubted you."

"Just don't do it again," I reply, and reach down to grab her ass, tilting her up so I can sink farther into her, grinding against her, and making us both see stars. The orgasm moves fast down my spine and through me, and the next thing I know, we're tangled up together in my bed, trying to catch our breath.

Finally, she shifts next to me and cups my cheek in her hand.

"This wasn't how I expected us to spend the day, but you'll get no complaints from me."

"Good." I smile and tuck her against me, kissing the crown of her head. "I need you to promise me something."

"Okay."

"If you have questions, ask me. I'll never lie to you, Riley. We can't have any doubts between us, especially if we're going to make a go of this after I go back to L.A."

"You're right," she says as she traces patterns through the hair on my chest. "I promise to talk to you before I jump to conclusions."

"Thank you."

"What are you going to do about Angie?"

"I don't know," I reply honestly. "There's a whole group of guys who play with me, and know her as well as I do, but I'll talk with them. I don't want to kick her out of the group without giving them a heads-up."

She nods. "I don't like feeling jealous. It's new to me."

"You're not normally a jealous woman?"

"Not at all," she says. "That's something that used to bother some of the guys I dated. They'd try to play games with me, thinking I'd get jealous and go running back to them, but that doesn't work on me. I guess I never cared enough about any of them to feel threatened or jealous."

"Why is it different now?"

"It just is." She's quiet as she gathers her thoughts. "I'll never be a crazy jealous person."

"Good, because that's a lot of drama."

"Exactly. I don't do well with drama. I don't need or want it in my life. My mom was always a dramatic person, and it drove me nuts."

"Are you not close to her?"

"Not really. I mean, it's not like we don't speak or anything, but we also don't have Sunday dinners together. I see her a few times a year."

I nod, loving that I continue to learn more and more about her.

I've fallen in love with her.

"You were mad," she says, and smiles up at me. "That was interesting."

"Not at you," I reply. "I was frustrated and pissed at Angie. I don't know what her deal is, but she's about to be very disappointed."

Riley sighs and nuzzles my chin with her nose. "I'm hungry."

"Me too. What do you want me to feed you?"

"What do you have?"

I take a quick mental inventory of the kitchen and wince. "Nothing that I could whip together into something edible."

She nods thoughtfully. "We could order in."

"Given our current state of undress, and that I don't plan to let you get dressed again, that's our only option."

"Should we order pizza again and I can shock the shit out of the delivery kid?"

I narrow my eyes and growl. "No. No, we shouldn't."

"Possessive much?"

"Did you completely miss the last hour?" I ask, and bite her shoulder. "Perhaps I should go over it again."

She laughs and then moans when I suck her nipple into my mouth.

"Oh yeah, I need a refresher course."

"I thought you were hungry?"

"We'll eat later."

Chapter Eleven

~Riley~

So, the film crew gets Veterans Day off?" Cami asks a few days later. We're in the office, looking at our schedule for the next week.

"Yep," I reply with a shrug.

"Are they all veterans?" Addie asks.

"No, but the network will have to pay them double time because of their union if they work today, so they said no work today."

"Wow, it's a good thing our people don't have a union," Cami says. "We pay them well as it is."

"It gives Mia a break in the kitchen," I reply, and scan my planner. "She's been filming every day, and then working through the evenings."

"She's exhausted," Addie says, shaking her head. "We're going to have to have another intervention with her."

"The last one didn't work," I reply, feeling just as frustrated with Mia, and the crazy amount of hours she puts in. "Seduction is her life."

"Yes, it is," Mia says as she walks through the door. "Stop talking about me. I'm fine. I'm not exhausted or burned out."

"Yet," Cami says. "You need a break."

"Tell it to Riley." Mia points at me and rolls her eyes. "She's the one who has her boyfriend barking orders at me and making me whip up extra food for cameras all day. The rest of you just had to do interviews. I have to cook for them."

"I guess I didn't consider that you'd have so much extra filming time," I concede with a wince. "I'm sorry about that."

"It's fine. They'll be gone in a week, and I can have my normal life back."

Everyone's quiet now, staring at me, and I look behind me as if there's someone else standing there. "Why are you all staring at me?"

"Because they'll be gone in a week," Cami says gently. "And that means Trevor will be gone too."

"I'm not thinking about it," I reply. "Let's look at the schedule for next week."

"Let's talk about Trevor leaving," Mia says instead. "Honestly, honey, are you okay?"

No, I'm not fucking okay.

But rather than fall apart in a tantrum, I smile and nod.

"I'm going to be just fine. We're not breaking up. Besides, we still have a week, so let's not dwell on it yet. You can wipe my tears next week."

"Shit," Mia says with a scowl. "There are going to be tears. I'm not particularly good with tears."

"And yet you're so good at consoling us through them," Addie says with a smile.

We spend the next twenty minutes talking about the schedule with the filming crew next week, and then I walk out of the office, headed toward the bar so I can check in with Kat.

"There you are!"

"Nana?" I spin around, shocked to see my nana sitting at a nearby table with Trevor. She's wearing her pearls, which I know she only does when she's on a fancy date.

I hurry over and kiss Nana on the cheek and sit in the empty seat next to her, across from Trevor, who's holding my gaze with happy green eyes.

"What are you two up to?"

"Well, this handsome gentleman caller asked me to join him for lunch. You know I couldn't pass up that offer."

"Absolutely not," I agree with a smile, and Trevor winks at me.

"I haven't been in here since you expanded," Nana says as she takes it all in. "It's truly beautiful, Riley."

"Thank you. Cami worked with a designer, so I can't take any of the credit, but we are very proud of it."

"Honey," Nana says as she covers my hand with hers, "I hope it doesn't bother you that I made a move on your man. I promise, it's strictly platonic."

I want to bust out laughing, and I can see that her eyes

are full of humor as well, but I manage to keep a straight face, and shift my head side to side as if I'm giving it thought.

"I guess that lunch isn't a big deal."

"Exactly, dear, it's only lunch. And I'm double his age."

"Age is a state of mind," Trevor murmurs, still watching me through his sexier-than-hell glasses. "And you're a joy to be with, Miss Dolores. I'm happy that you could join me on my day off."

I don't even know what to say. He's *voluntarily* hanging out with my nana on his day off.

I mean, who does that?

"I'll let you get back to your date," I say as I pat Nana's hand. "I have a full day today."

"Okay, dear."

And just like that, I've been dismissed. My nana is hilarious. Trevor leans in to talk to her, listening intently as she tells him an animated story.

I walk into the bar and look back, as if I still don't quite believe what I just saw.

"That's pretty sweet," Kat says as she joins me and wraps her arm around my shoulders. "Did you ask him to take her out today?"

"No." I shake my head, not able to look away as Trevor laughs at something Nana says, and then starts to relay his own funny anecdote. "I had no idea he was going to bring her here, or hang out with her at all, actually."

"Wow," Kat says with a sigh. "It's amazing how this guy is making an effort to connect with the person who means the most to you in the whole world."

When she says it like that, it brings tears to my eyes.

"I'm falling in love with him," I whisper, and brush a tear off my cheek. "Is that what you want me to say?"

"Not to me," she says, and kisses my cheek. "But I think you should say something to him sooner or later."

"Sooner or later," I agree. "Come on, we have work to do."

"I had another bartender quit, so we need to talk about placing another damn ad," she says as I take a seat at the bar. "Why can't I keep people? You guys don't have problems with staff in the restaurant."

"Maybe it's harder with bartenders?" I ask. "Not to mention, there is a lot of information to remember here, with your extensive wine list. So not just anyone will do."

"I know. Let's rework the wording of the ad, and I'll put some feelers out for a sommelier that might need a job as well."

"That fancy word sounds like they'll be expensive. Cami won't be happy with that."

"Well, I'm not happy about hiring people who don't have any experience and they quit in less than a month. That's a waste of money."

"I agree. I've added it to my list."

I scribble more notes in my planner. I can't help but wonder how things are going with Trevor and Nana, but I resolve to let them be, and concentrate on work. It's good that the camera crew isn't here today; it gives us all a chance to catch up and regroup.

There will be time for Trevor later.

IT'S BEEN ONE hell of a day.

I feel like today was for me what that crappy Monday was for Trevor last week. The weekly-special ad in the newspaper was wrong, one of our waitstaff quit, and a customer threw up all over their table.

Why would someone go out to eat when they know they have the flu? I mean, anniversary or not, that's just common sense.

So, rolling into the house at roughly eight in the evening isn't a surprise at all. I called Trevor on the way home, and told him that I'd just go to bed tonight. I need some quiet, and although I love being with him, I also need to start getting used to *not* being with him.

As I was reminded earlier today, he leaves next week.

And that just makes me sad.

My little house is dark and silent as I walk inside and hang my coat up along with my handbag and toss my keys in the bowl.

My stomach growls.

"Fucking hell, I'm hungry." I sigh and rub my forehead. I forgot to eat before I left. But I was just ready to get out of there. I love our business fiercely, but today was one of those days when I couldn't get out of there fast enough.

I hope I still have some ice cream in the freezer. That'll have to be good enough for dinner. I know I don't have anything to cook, even if I had the energy for it, which I don't.

I'm kind of pathetic.

I hurry back to the bedroom and change my clothes, feeling better in some loose yoga pants, no bra, and an old T-shirt. I throw my hair up in a high ponytail and wander out to the kitchen to go through the small pile of mail on the countertop.

Bill.

Credit-card offer.

Nordstorm flyer.

And that's about it.

Well, that chore is done.

I lean back on the counter and look around. Is it always this quiet here? Am I cold? Maybe a little. I should turn up the heat.

I should eat something.

Why am I so . . . *lost*?

I'm pulling on my bottom lip, trying to decide what in the hell to do now, when my doorbell rings.

And there on the other side of the door is Trevor, holding food boxes and a bouquet of flowers.

"Hi," he says with a smile. "I know you want a quiet night in, and I'm down for that too. I just didn't want to be without you tonight. We have a limited number of nights left."

"Don't remind me," I reply, and step back to let him in.

"Are you mad that I came when you told me not to?"

I shake my head. "No. This is much better."

He sets everything on the kitchen counter and I immediately walk into his arms, hugging him tightly. His big hands brush up and down my back, making me want to purr.

"Are you okay?"

I bite my lip, not wanting to cry and not entirely sure *why* I feel the urge to cry.

"I'm okay."

"Bad day?"

"Shittiest day in a long time." I sigh and kiss his chest, right over his heart, then press my ear there and listen to it thump and close my eyes when his arms tighten around me.

"Have you eaten?"

"No."

"Good. I brought Italian food."

"Carbs." I grin and hug him even tighter. I love carbs.

"I even brought tiramisu."

"You're the best ever."

He chuckles and kisses the crown of my head.

"And no Italian meal is complete without flowers."

"You're very nice to me." I tip my head back and look up into his green eyes. "And it's appreciated."

"I know." He kisses me lightly, then pulls away so he can start unloading the food that smells better than anything I've ever smelled.

Don't tell Mia.

"Dessert in the fridge," he murmurs, then pulls down plates and dishes us up.

"Wait, it's Wednesday night."

"It is," he agrees.

"Tonight is game night."

"Not tonight." He shrugs and licks his thumb, and just like that, my mind immediately goes to sexy time. "I told the guys I had plans, which I do, and I still need to decide how I'm going to handle the Angie situation. In the meantime, I'm going to spend as much time as I can with you."

"I like that plan."

I lead him to my couch and we both dig into our food. My chicken Parmesan is amazing.

"Thanks for the food. I was starving."

"Why didn't you eat at work?"

"Today just sucked and I wanted to get out of there. And, I forgot." I take another bite and sigh in happiness. "So good."

"So, what are we watching tonight? Vampires?"

I smile and wrinkle my nose. "You don't want to watch vampires."

"I don't mind." He shrugs one shoulder. "I'll watch whatever you're in the mood for. I'm surprised you didn't go to Cami's to watch your shows."

"We both had long days," I reply, and take a bite of still-warm bread. "We had some work to catch up on since we had a break from filming."

"I'm sorry that this has added more work for you," he says. "I didn't want that."

"I know. It's not forever, and we got a lot accomplished today."

"Well, you name it and we will watch it, m'lady."

"Okay, let's watch some vampires." I grin and turn on the television, then snuggle up next to him, still eating my food. "Before I forget, how's Nana? I was pretty surprised to see you together."

"I like her," he says. "She's an interesting person, and I had a free day, so I thought we would both enjoy a day out."

"She loved it," I reply. "She texted me and sent me a selfie."

"She had me help her put that selfie on her Facebook."

"Or, as she calls it, *the* Facebook."

"Yes." He laughs and finishes his pasta, setting his plate aside. "She's a hoot, and I'm glad you have her."

"Me too. Thank you." I set my plate aside with his and curl into him while we watch television. It's the perfect quiet evening.

It's amazing because we don't really have to do anything and I feel so much better when he's here than when he's not. As soon as his arms fold around me, he calms me.

I've never felt anything like it in my life.

And I'm quickly becoming addicted to it.

To him.

My God, what am I going to do when he leaves?

I take a deep breath and will myself not to think about it yet. We still have a whole week, and a lot can happen in that time.

Just enjoy him. Don't overthink it.

Of course, that's easier said than done.

My eyes are heavy, and before long the feel of a very solid and warm Trevor next to me lulls me into sleep.

SOMEONE IS CARRYING me.

Or I'm dreaming, but either way, it feels lovely.

"Shh," Trevor whispers in my ear. "I didn't mean to wake you."

"I love it when you carry me." My voice is small with slumber.

"I know." He kisses my brow and sets me on the edge of the bed. "Do you want to sleep in the clothes you're wearing?"

"Yeah, it's fine."

I could sleep in a sumo suit right now. I haven't been this sleepy in a long time. So I lie down on the bed, but then I'm lifted again.

"I have to turn the bed down," he says with a smile.

"Okay."

He gets me all settled in the bed, and through only one open eye, I watch him strip out of his clothes, the moonlight shining on his perfect body, and join me, pulling me to him the way he always does.

The man never stops touching me, and frankly, it's fucking amazing.

"Thank you," I whisper to him.

"For what?"

I love talking in the dark with hushed voices. It feels intimate, like we're telling secrets, even if we're not.

"For everything you did tonight. And for today with my nana. You're pretty great."

"I have moments," he says.

"I'm glad you came tonight."

"I'm glad you're glad."

He brushes my hair off my neck and kisses me there. It's not in an overtly sexual way. Just in a familiar, sweet way that makes my heart smile.

I'm so in love with this man it hurts.

"I sleep better when you're here," I whisper, and bite my lip. I want to tell him I've fallen in love with him, but I think it's too soon.

"Good because I plan on sleeping with you for a very long time, sweetheart."

Good lord, the man can use his words.

His arms are around me, he's pressed against my back, and I'm just not so sleepy anymore.

All he has to do is lightly kiss my damn neck and I'm so turned on I can't think straight.

I certainly can't sleep in this state.

And I don't have to because he's still *here*.

"Trevor?" I whisper, in case he's fallen asleep already.

"Yes, Riley?"

Thank God he hasn't fallen asleep.

"Are you overly tired?"

"Can you feel my cock pressed against your ass?" he asks, rather than answer my question.

"Yes."

I'm suddenly on my back and looking up into Trevor's eyes, illuminated by the moonlight.

"You were so tired I thought I'd just let you sleep."

"I appreciate the offer," I reply while dragging my hands down his side. He's made himself at home, nestled between my thighs. His dick is pressing against my center, and every damn nerve ending is on fire.

I tilt my hips up and smile up at him.

"You're awake now," he murmurs as he nudges the tip inside of me, making me gasp lightly.

"Wide-awake," I confirm. "And holy shit, that feels good."

"Yeah?" He pushes in farther and leans down to kiss me. "How about this?"

"So damn good," I reply. "It always feels so good."

He closes his eyes and begins to move in and out, in the perfect rhythm, keeping me right on the edge of falling over into a blinding orgasm.

He's doing it on purpose, and I want to beg him to stop and never to stop all at the same time.

"You're so fucking incredible," he breathes against my lips. "I always crave you. Whether you're with me or not, I fucking *need* you."

"So good with words," I whisper, and bear down, clutching on to him and watching in delight as his jaw tightens and every muscle in his body clenches with his orgasm.

As he's still shuddering, he presses his thumb to my clit, and I cry out as I come with him, every piece of me completely in love with him.

He collapses beside me, always careful to keep his weight off me. When I can form complete sentences again, I need to tell him he needn't bother.

I love feeling him over me.

As I float back to earth, I realize my eyes are heavy again.

"Sleep," Trevor whispers sweetly. "Go to sleep."

Chapter Twelve

~Trevor~

*Y*ou did great, Trev," my boss, Mark, says happily in my ear. "Wrapping early is great, and makes up for the holiday day we lost last week. The footage you've sent is great. It's going to be a good show."

"I think so too," I reply, and wave as the sound guy leaves. "Hey, I'm going to stick around in Portland for a few extra days."

"Why?"

I take a deep breath.

"Because I need some vacation time," I reply, not lying in the least. "It's been a few years."

"How much time are we talking about?"

"I'm going to be here through next week. I'll be back in my office the following Monday."

"A whole week." His voice has lost the excitement of a

few moments ago. "I was hoping to go over some new show ideas next week."

"I'm sorry, Mark, but it'll have to wait. I wasn't due to be back in the office until late next week anyway, so this is only a few extra days."

"You're right," he says with a sigh. "You have the apartment until Wednesday morning. You can have my assistant arrange for you to keep it."

"I'll be checking out early."

"Trevor, what's going on?"

"Nothing at all, just taking some time for myself."

"Okay. I'll see you when you get back."

I end the call and have a brief chat with the camera guy, then go in search of the girls.

Mia is, naturally, in the kitchen.

"Can you take a ten-minute break?" I ask her, earning a glare.

"Give me a few," she says.

"Great, meet me in your office."

She nods, going right back to whatever she's working on on the stove top.

Kat and Cami are in the bar.

"I need to borrow you guys. Can we please meet in the office?"

"Sure," Cami says as Kat turns to her employee and tells her to let Kat know if she needs anything.

"Where are Addie and Riley?" I ask.

"In the office," Kat says.

"Perfect." I lead the ladies into the office, and each of

them immediately sits at her respective desk. They're beautiful women, and not a little intimidating when they're all seated in the office.

"Mia's on her way," I inform them.

"Are we in trouble?" Addie asks with a smirk.

"On the contrary," I reply just as Mia hurries in.

"You've got five minutes," she says impatiently.

"That's all I'll need." I rub my hands together as my gaze travels to each woman. "I have excellent news. We've wrapped shooting."

"What?" Cami says with a frown. "I thought we had to film through Tuesday."

"We got everything we need," I reply. "Today's interviews were the last of it. I've already sent the rest of the crew home."

"It's convenient that you wrapped on a Friday," Cami says with a nod.

"I don't mean to be rude," Mia says with a smile, "but thank God."

"You all did so great." I hold each of their gazes with mine, speaking in earnest. "Seriously, you couldn't have been better. My boss is already very pleased."

"Good." Riley finally speaks up, avoiding my gaze now. "I'm happy to hear it was successful."

"I think we're going to miss having you around," Kat says. "We should have a party to celebrate!"

"Absolutely," Addie says with a nod. "We should have it at my place. There's plenty of space for everyone. I can call Jake and have him get the ball rolling for tonight, if that works for everyone."

"That's short notice," Mia says.

"We have people," Addie says, waving Mia off. "I expect to see you all at my place, tonight, around seven."

"Okay." Mia stands and rubs her neck. "I'll call in an extra cook and duck out early."

"Wow," Kat says, raising a brow. "You didn't even put up much of a fight."

"You're very funny," Mia says, and walks out of the office. All of the girls stand, each of them shaking my hand as they leave. Riley's hung back, and as she approaches me, I block the path to the door.

"Can we talk for a minute?"

"Okay," she says, and backs up, leaning on the front of her desk.

"How do you feel?"

"Peachy." Her smile is fake. "It's just fantastic that you're leaving early."

"Is that what you think? No." I move to her and take her shoulders in my hands. "I'm not leaving early. I'm actually staying longer."

She frowns and seems to sag in relief, all at the same time.

"How long?" she asks softly.

"Until the following Monday."

She nods, her face flushing. "I'm ridiculously relieved."

"I'm sorry, sweetheart, I didn't mean to upset you."

"I'm fine," she says, but I can see through her. And I get it. I'm not ready to say good-bye either.

"I'm going to need a place to stay."

Her lips twitch in humor. "There are plenty of hotels in Portland."

"True." I nod and pull her against me, letting her feel the length of me against her. "But that wouldn't be nearly as nice as seeing you whenever I like."

"You have a point." Her hands travel up my arms and around my neck. "I guess it wouldn't be so bad to share my things with you for a bit."

"That's very generous."

"You'll have to earn your keep," she says, her voice very serious. God, she makes me laugh.

"Of course." I purse my lips, trying to keep a straight face. "You know I can cook, so there's that."

"There's that," she agrees.

"I'm handy with laundry."

"That's a bonus," she says with a smile. "I hate laundry."

"I kind of enjoy it, actually."

"Well, then by all means, feel free to do laundry."

I smirk. "What else can I do for you?"

Her hand glides down my chest and she cups my dick in her hand, immediately waking it up. "I have a few ideas."

"I love your ideas."

"I haven't even told you what they are yet," she says with a laugh.

"I can already tell your ideas are awesome."

"You'd be right. When are you moving in?"

"I was thinking I'd go back and pack up now while you finish up work."

She shocks me by wrapping her arms around me and hugging me tightly.

"I have a rock hide-a-key by the front porch," she mumbles into my chest. "Just go make yourself at home."

"Are you sure?" I tip her chin up so I can see into her blue eyes. "If you'd rather I kept the apartment, I can do that."

"I'd rather have you with me, for as long as I can."

I cup her face and kiss her until we're both breathless.

"Thank you. I'll see you tonight."

"And don't forget about our wrap party tonight. You should invite the crew."

We used a Portland-based camera and sound crew rather than fly everyone up from L.A. and pay for their lodging and meals on top of salary.

"I'm sure they'd like that. I'll let them know."

"Okay." She smiles as she steps away from me. "Now leave before I strip you naked and have my way with you on my desk."

Her lips are wet and parted, her hair twisted up nicely, just begging to be tousled by my fingers. I can't resist leaning in and pressing my nose to her neck. She shivers beautifully.

"That's not much of a threat, Riley."

She laughs and buries her fingers in my hair. "I really don't have time for this."

"Yes, you do," I reply, letting my hand slide up her bare thigh beneath her skirt. "You own the fucking business."

"That door is unlocked," she warns me. Her head falls

back with a sigh as my fingers find home plate. "Someone could walk in."

"I don't seem to give a fuck." But I'm blocking the view from the door with my back as I push her onto her desk. I'm not going to fuck her, not right now, but I'm going to make damn sure she spends the rest of the day thinking of me.

"Trevor," she breathes. She's holding on to my arms, her nails biting my flesh through my shirt. "Oh my God."

"That's right, sweetheart." I bite her earlobe and then press my lips to her ear. "Come. Right now, Riley."

She obeys without a moment's pause, clinging to me, her pussy contracting around my fingers.

"You're so damn gorgeous."

"You're good at that," she replies, swallowing thickly. "My turn."

"Nope." I lick my fingers clean and then straighten her skirt and back away. My cock is pulsing like a motherfucker, but we're both going to have to wait until later. "I'll see you later."

"Should I say thanks?" she asks with a laugh.

"That works." I kiss her, hard, then walk out of the office whistling. I ignore the smirks from Cami and Addie, sending them a wave as I walk out of the restaurant.

I have some packing to do.

THE GIRLS ARE dancing in the middle of the room. Jake and Addie's house—"mansion" is a better word—is massive, and the perfect place to accommodate so many people.

Two of our crew showed up as well. I think they were just curious to get a look at Jake Knox's house, as they're both big fans, and Jake has stayed away from the restaurant while we filmed, wanting to maintain his privacy.

They're both standing with him now while he holds his baby girl, chatting and laughing.

"They're something," Landon says beside me, pointing at our girls. "They've done this since they were kids."

"You've known them for a long time," I reply, and take a sip of my beer while I watch Riley move out of rhythm in her skintight red dress.

Fuck me, she looks amazing in it.

"Most of our lives," Landon says.

"Did you always have a crush on Cami?" Mac, Kat's fiancé, asks.

"I started to notice her as something other than my sister's friend when I was in high school. We've always been good friends, and when we got older, the chemistry was off the charts."

"But you never pursued her?" I ask.

"I went to college, and then into the navy," Landon says, shaking his head. "She got married. We went in two different directions."

"Until last year," Mac says.

"Yep. She's the best thing that's ever happened to me."

"I know what you mean," Mac says, staring at Kat. "I wasn't looking for her, but there she was, terrified on that plane."

He goes on to tell me about how Kat has a phobia of flying, and he was sitting next to her on a flight down to California.

"All of these women are impressive," I add, and smile when Riley spins, almost crashing right into Cami. "Riley has no rhythm."

"She never did," Landon says with a laugh. "But she doesn't care. You have to admire that about her."

I love her for a million different reasons.

"Do you love her?" Landon asks me, catching my attention. "Riley?"

"No, Mother Teresa. Yes, Riley."

I take a sip of my drink. "I don't know if I should answer that question when I haven't even told *her* how I feel about her."

"As long as you're not just in it for the sex, I'm fine," Landon says. "Because she's not really that kind of person."

"I know," I reply with a smile. "She told me early on, and we are exclusive."

"Great." Landon waves at Cami, who's waving at him from her dancing spot.

The song ends, and the girls scatter, each going to her man. Mia pours herself another drink.

"Hi," Riley says happily.

"Hello there, beautiful."

Her chest is heaving from being out of breath, highlighting those sexy tits, and I can't stand not having my hands on her anymore.

"I'd like to speak with you," I murmur to her, taking her

hand in mine and leading her out of the room and down the hallway to a bathroom.

I shut the door behind us and pin her against the wall.

"What's wrong?" she asks.

"Not a fucking thing." I kiss her forehead. "Watching you dance in that dress just about undid me."

"You're drunk," she says with a giggle.

"Nope," I reply. "Unless you count being drunk on you."

"So, do you want to go at it in here? Because I've never been a fan of bathroom sex."

"No?" I cock a brow and let my hands glide down her sides to the hem of her dress. Her legs are bare beneath it, as they were earlier, and I'm happy to discover she's not wearing panties. "What don't you like about it?"

"It's rather unsanitary, isn't it?" She wrinkles her nose, then bites her lip when my fingertip drags up the crease of her leg, right next to where it meets her sex.

"I'm quite sure that Addie and Jake have a diligent housekeeper," I reply, and plant my mouth on her neck, just below her ear, as my finger finds her clit.

"I don't remember her name," Riley whispers.

"I don't give a fuck," I reply, and slip my finger through her wetness and into her. Her leg is wrapped around my waist, begging me to go deeper, to free my hard, pulsing cock and take her, right here.

But I'm not going to.

"Trevor," she moans, and I cover her lips with my fingers.

"Shh," I croon, and gently bite her collarbone. "We don't want someone to hear you."

"The music is loud," she replies, and fists her fingers in my hair. "I want you."

"Best words ever," I growl, and add a finger inside of her, making a *"come here"* motion, and watch as I bring her close to the brink of orgasm. "Do you know how fucking beautiful you are?"

Her eyes are closed as she bites her lip and shakes her head back and forth.

"Your body comes alive under my touch. It's the most amazing thing in the world to watch."

"It's pretty great to feel too," she says. Her voice is hoarse and full of lust.

Just as she's about to fall over the ledge, I pull away. Her eyes are glassy as she frowns at me. "Where are you going?"

"Back out to the party. You don't like bathroom sex, remember?"

"You've changed my mind. Besides, you can't do this to me twice in one day. It's cruel."

"You came twice," I remind her, but she shakes her head.

"That's only part of it," she says. "I get off on getting *you* off."

My cock has never been this hard.

Her cheeks are flushed beautifully, her nipples hard against her dress.

I lean in and kiss her cheek, and then her earlobe.

"Later," I whisper, and take her hand, leading her back out to join the others.

"Now," she replies, and quickly frees my cock from my

pants. She squats and immediately takes me into her mouth, and if I were a younger man, I'd come on the spot.

As it is, she uses both hands and that mouth of hers that was made for sin, and I'll be damned if I can hold back any longer.

I come fast, right into her mouth. She swallows and smiles, then stands and tucks me back in my pants.

"There. Now we can wait for later to get down to business."

She winks and leads me back to the party.

"Oh, good, you're back," Kat says when she sees Riley. "I was just telling Mac about that time in college that we took that road trip down to San Francisco."

"Oh lord, that was the worst trip ever," Riley says, rolling her eyes.

"Are you okay?" Cami asks, tilting her head. "You look a little flushed."

Riley smiles and shrugs one shoulder. "I think the alcohol is kicking in."

She hasn't even finished her first drink, but we'll keep that secret between us. Riley sits next to Addie, who's now holding the baby.

"We had three flat tires on that trip," Riley says as I take a seat next to her. "We were stranded on Mount Shasta for almost twenty-four hours."

"Did you all go?" Landon asks. "I don't remember this story."

"No, it was just Kat and me," Riley says. "And neither of us knew how to change a tire."

"I'm a genius," Kat reminds us all with a smile. "I knew *how,* I just didn't *want* to."

"What she said," Riley says with a shrug. I glance around the room, noticing that the two crew members have left.

"Hey, man," Jake says to me, "thanks for being so understanding about not asking me to interview for the show."

"It's not a problem," I reply. "This show is about the restaurant, and if you want to remain private, that's your right."

"Not everyone is so understanding," Addie says, rolling her eyes. Riley holds her hands out to the baby, who happily leans toward her, drooling like crazy.

"Aw, are you teething, little princess?" Riley kisses the baby's cheek. "You look more like your mama every day."

"Thank God," Jake says, looking at both his girls with love written all over his face.

"You're so smitten," Cami says to him. "It's awesome."

"How could I not be? Have you seen them?"

"They are beautiful," Kat says with a smile. "You guys just keep having babies, because I'm not going to. I'll spoil yours."

"We can do that," Jake says, earning a glare from his wife. "Not *today.*"

"You're damn right not today," Addie says as the baby starts to fuss. "I love this little love, but she's a handful all on her own. I think it's her bedtime."

"I'll take her up," Jake says. He retrieves the baby and takes her out of the room.

The girls start discussing the restaurant, and I rub light

circles on Riley's back, working my way lower and lower until I can feel the top of her crack and let my hand rest there, tickling. Her voice skips in whatever it is she's saying and she tosses me a look, then returns to her conversation.

I want to keep her in a constant state of arousal all evening. My hand roams to her thigh. She has her legs crossed, and her bare knee is practically begging for attention. I let my hand rest on her thigh for a few minutes, and just when she seems to calm down, I tighten my grip, slide my fingers to her knee, and watch in amusement as goose bumps erupt along her perfect skin.

"So, now that the crew is gone, how have you enjoyed Portland, Trevor?" Mac asks from across the room. Kat is in his lap, cuddling into him with a very satisfied grin on her face.

"It's a beautiful city," I reply honestly. "The food is great. The company has been even better."

I smile down at Riley, who blushes.

"It's no secret that I've been seeing Riley."

"Definitely no secret," Cami says with a grin. "But I think it was good of you to keep it pretty professional whenever we were filming."

"I'm not an idiot, and I'm not willing to give the crew any reason to gossip about any of us. News travels quickly, as I'm sure you know."

"It's a wise move," Landon says with a nod.

"So, I've decided to stay for a few extra days," I continue, watching Riley as I speak. My thumb is still wreaking havoc on her knee. "I'd like to spend as much time with Riley as I can before I head back to L.A."

"That's sweet," Cami says. "You make a really beautiful couple."

I smile at Riley and sweep her dark blond hair over her shoulder and off her neck, which I know drives her crazy.

Women have a thing about having their necks touched. It's their Kryptonite.

Riley takes a deep breath and smiles at Cami.

"Thank you. It's his glasses. They're sexy."

"I'm quite sure it's simply you," I reply, and lean in to place a kiss on her neck, discreetly licking her and making all of the hair on her body stand up.

She's so bloody turned on, it's fascinating.

We spend the next few hours talking with the others before we say our good-byes and are in my car on the way back to her house.

She's uncharacteristically quiet, turned toward the window and watching the streetlights as they whip by on the freeway.

I reach over to touch her knee, but she jerks out of my reach and glares at me.

"No."

I cock a brow. "No?"

"No. You've been torturing me for *hours.* Do you have any idea how fucking uncomfortable I am right now?"

"Oh yeah, it's straining against my jeans, sweetheart."

"Good." She turns back to the window and sits in silence until we get to her house. She storms out of the car and through the front door, me right on her heels. "I'm going to take a shower."

"Great idea." I smile and follow her back to her bedroom, but she stops and whirls, rounding on me.

"Alone, Trevor. I'm going to take a *cold* shower, alone."

"Fuck that."

Chapter Thirteen

~Riley~

My entire body has been humming for the better part of three hours, damn him. It's agony. He's grinning down at me like he's won the motherfucking lottery, and I want to smack him.

So, I turn and march into the bathroom, turn on the shower, and strip out of my dress, watching him while I do it.

He's kept me frustrated all evening, he can have a turn.

"You're so fucking beautiful," he says as he watches me shed my bra and turn to the shower. He's next to me in three quick strides, but rather than touch my boobs or anything farther south, he simply kisses me. Chastely. Intimately.

Damn him.

"Get in the shower, Riley."

He watches me as I step into my glass-enclosed shower and under the water. It's hot, too hot for my already warm skin, so I bring the temperature down. I turn away from Trevor and reach for the soap, but before I can do anything else, he's joined me, naked as the day he was born.

He's also shed his glasses.

"I don't remember extending an invitation," I say, but rather than reply, he simply takes the soap from my hand, lathers up his own hands, and makes a circle motion with his finger, implying that he'd like for me to turn around. "I'm still mad at you."

His lips twitch in humor. "I'm about to make it up to you."

I turn away and he immediately begins to rub my back with his soap-slick hands, thoroughly kneading my muscles in the most delicious way.

The man's hands are *everything*.

"How is this?"

"If you stop, I'll never speak to you again."

He chuckles and continues to rub down to the small of my back, over my ass cheeks and up the crack, and I immediately remember him tickling me earlier at Addie's.

"I had no idea my ass crack was an erogenous zone."

"Hmm," is his only reply as his hands come around my torso to lather up my belly and breasts. My nipples are still puckered from hours' worth of torment. "Your body is ridiculously perfect."

I smirk, but don't say anything. I know I'm not perfect, but I love that he thinks I am. He's the best boost to my ego I've ever had, bless him.

After he's lathered me all up, I move to step under the water, but he stops me.

"This is my job."

He takes the removable nozzle off the wall and sprays me down, letting all of the soap wash away. Rather than replace the shower head, he backs me up until my back is pressed to the cold tile.

"Now, let's see if we can change your mind about shower sex."

His green eyes are eating me alive as the water runs in little rivers over my skin. He urges me to lift my leg and rest my foot on the built-in bench, and before I can do anything else, my shower head is pressed to my clit and he's turned the setting to *pulse*.

"Holy fucking shit," I mutter, and let my head fall back against the tile as zings of electricity shoot from my clit and down my arms and legs. If he doesn't let me come this time, I'll fucking kill him.

"How is this?" he asks.

"Holy fucking shit," I repeat, making him smile triumphantly.

"Your face is so damn expressive during sex," he says, as if he's talking about the sports page in the newspaper. "I can't get enough of you."

"Jesus, Trevor, if you keep that up, I'll—"

"You'll what?"

I can't answer him. He's tilted the nozzle to the side, and the change in angle is making me see stars.

I don't think I can make my mouth work.

"You'll what?" he asks again.

"Fucking come," I reply with a pant.

"Yes, baby, go over for me."

Oh, thank Christ!

He reaches around me with his free hand and pushes two fingers inside me, and that's all it takes to send me flying into space, broken into a million pieces. Every muscle is quivering, every nerve ending on fire.

The water is gone now, turned off, and he's leading me out of the shower. He dries us both and leads me to the bed, and I can see that he has every intention of fucking me blind.

Which is great, but he's going to have to wait for it.

You know what they say, payback's a bitch. And for today, her name is Riley.

When he would guide me down on the bed, I press my hand on his chest and shake my head.

"You lie down," I instruct him. He narrows his eyes for a brief second, but he complies, lying on his back in the middle of the bed, spread out like a buffet for my pleasure.

And I plan to milk a lot of pleasure from this man.

He's already hard as a rock, which serves him right for keeping me on the edge of orgasm for the better part of four hours.

Then again, I've been freaking turned on since the moment I laid eyes on him.

"Are you going to join me?" he asks.

"Yes," I reply simply, and sink one knee into the bed beside him. "I want you to stay just like this."

"Feeling a bit dominant tonight?"

I just tilt my head and he smiles.

"Okay, I'll stay like this."

"Thank you." I kneel next to him, but don't touch him. My gaze sweeps from his head to his feet and back up again. There are plenty of scars, but no ink. His skin is smooth and bronze, still damp from the shower.

And God sure did bless him with incredible muscles. Seriously, all of this should be illegal.

Or come with a warning label.

"Are you just going to look?" he asks.

"No," I reply, and drag my fingertips down his torso. "I'm going to play for a bit. Is that okay?"

"Whatever you want," he says, making me smile.

"Perfect."

Without further ado, I lean over and take the head of his cock in my mouth. Trevor sucks his breath in through his teeth and his hands dive into my hair. I grip him firmly in my fist and move up and down in a slow, steady rhythm. Not fast or hard enough to make him come.

Not yet.

"Killing me," he groans.

I don't stop. I cup his balls with my free hand, and work him over for a while, enjoying the way everything in him, every muscle, tightens under my touch.

My phone rings.

Trevor growls.

I reach for it.

"You're answering?"

I smile sweetly and hit accept.

"Hi, Mia," I say cheerfully, and Trevor's eyes narrow menacingly.

I'm so going to pay for this.

I can't wait.

"Hey, I just wanted to ask you if you want the rest of us to pick up some of your work next week so you can spend more time with Trevor."

"That's incredibly thoughtful, Mia. I would love that. Should we meet on Monday so we can go through some things?"

"Sure, sounds good. Have a fun weekend with him. You deserve it, Riley."

My eyes haven't left him. He reaches down to take his dick in his hand, but I shake my head *no* and he rolls his eyes, but he obeys.

"I'll see you on Monday."

I hang up, toss the phone aside, and smile down at Trevor.

"Where was I?"

"You had your sexy-as-fuck mouth wrapped around my cock and I was getting very close to coming."

"Oh yeah. That." I grin down at him, and he moves fast, grabbing on to me and pinning me under him. He nudges his way between my thighs, and much to my delight, he sinks inside me, making us both moan.

"Finally," I whisper.

"We could have reached this point a lot faster if you hadn't been trying to kill me."

"What goes around comes around." I kiss his forearm. "You were trying to kill me all night."

"But what a way to go," he says with a laugh, and then there are no more words as he takes us both to paradise.

"So, I NEED a new outfit," I tell him the following morning as we walk through the mall together. "Mac is throwing a surprise party for Kat's birthday and it's a rockabilly theme. I would usually just raid her closet, but it's her party, so I can't."

"Okay, I'm game," he says, and kisses the back of my hand. "Do you have a place in mind?"

"Yep, there's a great spot here that Kat shops at all the time. We'll start there."

I lead him into the shop and we wander from rack to rack until I have five outfits to try on. The salesgirl leads us to the back of the store where the fitting rooms are, and Trevor sits on a chair while he waits for me to change.

The first outfit is a definite no, but I show him anyway.

"Take it off," he says immediately.

"You don't like it?" I turn to the mirror and scowl. "Yeah, this is a no."

"Don't ever put that on again," he says, shaking his head.

"Wow, you feel passionately about this. Okay, this is a no."

I return to the dressing room and change into the next outfit, which is *much* better. When I walk out to show him, his jaw drops and he just stares for a moment.

"Oh yeah, this is better."

"Absolutely not," he says with a scowl.

"What? It's cute!" I turn to the mirror and admire myself in the fun red dress. It hugs me in all the right places.

"It's too sexy," he says. "I won't be at this party to defend you from all of the other men."

"Uh, you do know that all of the other men are taken, right? Not to mention that *I'm* also taken."

"No way. Next."

I roll my eyes and go back into the room to change. This one, a pretty light blue dress with a white collar, might be the ticket.

"Much better," Trevor says with a nod. "Beautiful."

I turn to the mirror and smile. He's right, this one is classy and fun, perfect for a fun night with my friends.

"I like it too."

He walks up behind me and hugs me around the waist, lowering his head next to mine.

"This didn't take long."

"I'm a quick shopper," I reply, enjoying the way he feels pressed up behind me. "I'll change and pay for this and we can go."

"Great. I'll help."

He leads me back into the dressing room and kisses me breathless.

"We're in a dressing room," I hiss.

"Nothing slips past you," he says with a laugh. "Yes, we are."

"I'm not—"

"Excuse me, sir," the salesgirl says in a bored voice through the door. "You have to come out of there."

"We got caught," he says with a whisper, and wiggles his eyebrows. "We're a scandal."

"You're crazy."

"About you," he says, and kisses my cheek before opening the door to step out. "Sorry, she needed my help."

"Uh-huh," I hear the salesgirl say as she walks away.

"She's not amused," he says through the door.

"I wonder how many people try to have sex in these rooms?" I say.

"More than you want to know!" the salesgirl yells from the front of the store. "And sound travels in here."

I hear Trevor chuckle, and I can't help but join him as I zip up my jeans and gather my things. He's leaning against the doorframe, his arms crossed over his chest, when I open the door.

"Hi." I smile up at him and feel the butterflies stir in my belly when his eyes travel down to my breasts and back to my eyes.

"Hello. Would you like to accompany me home?"

I tilt my head back and forth, as if I'm giving it a lot of thought. "Okay."

"Had me guessing there for a minute," he says, and takes the dress out of my hands so he can link his fingers with mine. "Would have been embarrassing if you turned me down."

"Humiliating," I agree, and watch as the salesgirl rings me up, folds the dress, and stuffs it into a bag.

Before I can pass her my card, Trevor hands her his.

"You don't have to buy me this dress."

"I know." He kisses the top of my head and rubs a circle on my back. "I want to. It's really beautiful on you."

What did I do to deserve this man?

Oh yeah, I dated assholes for more than a decade.

I totally deserve him, and every moment of happiness that comes along with him.

He's carrying my bag, holding my hand, and leading me down the mall. We reach a gaming store, and he glances down at me.

"I'd like to stop in and see if there's a specific game that I can preorder."

"In Portland?"

"This store is in L.A. too," he says with a smile.

"Let's go, then." He leads me through many rows of games to the checkout counter and the kid who looks like he might have *just* gone through puberty standing behind it. They talk games, specifically the one Trevor wants to buy, and I'm lost in the language that seems to be specific to the gaming world.

Ten minutes later, we're walking back out and Trevor's game will be ready for him in L.A. in about a month.

"I know it's early, but I'm in the mood for some fro-yo," I say as we pass the do-it-yourself frozen yogurt place in the food court.

"It's always time for fro-yo," Trevor says with a grin. We make our way down the line, filling our paper bowls with the frozen treat and adding bits of chocolate, strawberries, marshmallows and whipped cream.

I glance up at Trevor when I put the whipped cream back in its slot. "This could be fun sometime," I say, eyeing the whipped cream.

"It's a date," he replies, and smirks as he leads me to the

counter so the young woman can weigh our bowls and he can pay.

We're quietly watching people pass by, eating our treat. The silence between us has always been comfortable. I love not feeling like I have to keep a steady stream of conversation going with this man.

He seems to need the same amount of quiet that I do.

"You have something right here." He points to the side of his own mouth, and I stick my tongue out to search for it.

"Did I get it?"

"No." He chuckles and reaches out to gently wipe some chocolate off the other corner of my mouth. I catch his wrist in my hand and lick the chocolate off his finger, making his eyes dilate. "Riley."

It's a warning or a plea, I'm not sure which. We've had so much sex in the past few weeks, it's a wonder that either of us can still walk.

Every muscle in my body is sore. It's a good sore, but it's intense.

Satisfying.

"Riley," he says again, and licks his lips.

"I didn't do anything," I reply innocently, and take a bite.

"You're not innocent," he says. "You can't even try to fool me, I know you too well already."

"Well, I may not be innocent, but I'm pretty, so there's that."

He laughs and tucks my hair behind my ear.

"You're not just pretty, you're beautiful. Inside and out."

Keep saying stuff like this, and I'll just keep falling right in love with you.

"You're good at words." I steal a gummy bear off the top of his yogurt and pop it in my mouth. "Did you take a class in college for speaking to girls?"

"No." He takes a strawberry from my dish and eats it. "I just think it's important to be honest and nice to the person you care about."

"Was that missing from your previous relationship?" I immediately regret asking the question. I really don't want to know too much about his marriage because every time I think about him being married to someone else, I get jealous.

Which is dumb because he didn't even know I existed when he married her.

And I didn't know *he* existed, which feels weird because it seems that I've known him forever.

"Sometimes," he says. "We weren't unkind to each other, but we didn't give each other what we needed either."

"What did you need?" I forget about my yogurt now, leaning in to hear him better.

He's quiet for a long minute, his eyes on his dish as he moves his spoon around in the yogurt, and finally he looks up at me with sad eyes. "I guess I just needed to be *seen*. To be respected, even when my interests were different from hers."

I nod slowly. "I can see that. I'm not trying to compare myself to her in any way—"

"You can't," he says, "you're nothing like her."

"Good. But I enjoy watching you game, or listening to you when you talk about it. I don't understand most of it, but it's fun to watch your eyes light up in excitement when you talk about it."

"I probably talk about it too much," he says with a sheepish smile. I reach over and take his hand in mine, giving it a squeeze.

"No, you don't. I may not play, but I want to hear your thoughts. It's fun."

He kisses my hand twice.

"You're a special woman, Riley."

"I'm glad you think so, but I think I'm just a decent human being who finally found another decent human being."

"And I'm happy that you found me," he says. "What do you want to do with the rest of our day?"

"As long as I'm with you, I don't care."

He stands and throws our empty bowls away, then holds his hand out for mine.

"Okay; well then, let's get started on it."

Chapter Fourteen

~Trevor~

Spending the past week with Riley has been unlike anything else I've ever known. We're just so *easy* together. If I need to be quiet, she's quiet too. Being in her company never gets old.

We're both on her couch the following Thursday evening. I'm playing on the Xbox with Scott and she's curled up beside me, reading.

"So what was up with Angie not showing up last night?" Scott asks.

I glance at Riley and kiss the crown of her head.

"Angie has decided to stir up some trouble," I reply, not uncomfortable in the least to talk about it in front of Riley, who glances up at me with a raised brow. "Scott's wondering why she wasn't in our group last night."

"What's going on?" he asks as we both kill zombies.

"Apparently, she's decided that she and I are a couple, and she warned Riley that I'm also unstable and am capable of hurting her."

"Hurting Angie?"

"No, hurting Riley."

"So, basically she's crazy," he says, and then curses when the zombies kill him. I run over to revive him.

"Crazy bitch," Riley mutters, making me grin. I like that she's a bit jealous. If she wasn't, she wouldn't be invested in this relationship.

And I'm pretty fucking invested.

"Why didn't you say something?" Scott asks.

"I didn't play with you guys last week."

"This happened *before* last week?" he demands, sounding more than a little indignant.

"I'm just not sure how I'm going to handle it. I mean, I don't have a problem not speaking to her, but we're a group, and I need to talk to all of you about it."

"Seriously, I don't think the other guys would have an issue if you suggested we didn't play with her anymore. That shit's not okay. It's not like you've *ever* dated her, or fucked her, or whatever."

"Angie's flaky," I reply. "She goes through men like underwear. If that's even true."

"I was just going to say that," Scott agrees. "Who knows how much of what she says is true? And frankly, I don't give a shit."

"You know," Riley says, laying her hand on my thigh, "I

don't really care if you play with her in the group. I would just hope that you don't play with her alone."

I smile down at this amazing woman, not even caring that a zombie just killed me. She's so fucking sweet.

"I don't think you should do either one," Scott says, clearly able to hear Riley.

"I don't either," I reply. "I don't appreciate her trying to fuck with my girl. She's a liar and a pot stirrer, and that just pisses me off."

"I get it," Scott says. "If she'd tried that shit with my wife, Wendy would have kicked her ass."

"I'm quite sure that Riley also wanted to kick Angie's ass."

"It could still happen," Riley whispers, making me grin.

"I love it when she gets a bit violent," I say to Scott, who chuckles.

"Are things going well, man?" he asks.

"Never better," I reply honestly. "I can't believe this week is almost over."

Riley keeps her head down, eyes pinned to her book, but I see her fingers turn white as she grips her iPad more tightly at my words.

I kiss her head again.

"I thought you were coming home today," he says.

"I extended the trip until Sunday afternoon. I have to be in the office Monday morning."

"We should go get a beer after you get back," Scott replies.

"Sure." We're quiet for a few minutes as the game intensifies and we concentrate on killing the enemy.

"This game is pretty violent," Riley says.

"Yeah, we have the gore turned up on high," I reply. "What's the point otherwise?"

"I'm not judging," she says, holding her hands up. "Just an observation."

"Does it bother you?"

"No, it's fascinating," she says. "I've watched you play this more than I've read this book. Maybe that means this book isn't so great."

"Or you're just enamored with me, and can't concentrate on anything else."

"It's too bad you don't have an ego," she says, and rolls her eyes. Scott laughs in my ear.

"She's funny. So what are you going to do about Angie?"

"I'll talk to the other guys next week, just to give them a heads-up, and then I'll probably send her a message and tell her to back off."

"Has she sent more messages lately?"

"Not to me." I frown and glance at Riley. "Has Angie sent you any more messages?"

"Just one," she says, and shrugs one shoulder as if it's no big deal.

"What? When? What did she say?"

"She sent it a couple days ago. Just said, '*I haven't heard from you, and want to make sure you received my message.*'"

"Did you reply?"

"Fuck no," Riley says with a scoff. "I don't know her, and I know you'll handle it."

"Good."

"And if you don't handle it," she continues, "I'll tell her to go fuck herself."

"I really like your new girl," Scott says.

"Yeah, she's our kind of people," I reply with a laugh. "Smitty just joined us. We'll kill more of these bastards now."

There's no more talk about crazy girls I hardly know, or my private life at all, as the three of us go through the motions of kicking ass.

When the game is over, I look over to find Riley fast asleep, her head on my bicep. Her iPad is resting in her lap, the screen black.

"I should go, guys," I tell them. "It's time for bed."

"Have fun," Scott says before he ends our group chat. I set the controller aside, turn off Riley's TV, and lift her in my arms to take her to bed.

Her eyes open immediately.

"I can walk. I'm not that out of it."

"I've got you," I reply, and kiss her cheek. "I want to carry you as much as possible while I still can."

"You're quite romantic," she says, and lays her head on my shoulder. "I like that about you."

I COME AWAKE the next morning and roll over to find Riley already watching me with bright blue eyes and a grin on her gorgeous mouth.

"Good morning," she says.

"Morning," I reply, and stretch, then reach for her. "I want to hold you for a bit, and then I'll go get us coffee."

"I want to go," she says with a grin. "Let me spoil you just a bit."

You spoil me every fucking day.

"If fetching coffee makes you happy, who am I to say no?"

"Exactly," she says, and kisses my jawline. "You're sexy in the morning, all rumpled and warm and sleepy."

"Hmm," I reply, and drag my hand down her naked spine. "Back at you."

She smiles and kisses my jaw again, then pulls away from me.

"Come back here."

Her eyes are sparkling with mischief as she shakes her head no. "I'm going to get us coffee."

She pulls on some Mickey Mouse yoga pants, a purple T-shirt that says MONDAYS ARE FOR AMATEURS and yellow flip-flops.

No bra. No panties.

She twists her hair up into a messy knot, and throws a red hoodie over the ensemble.

"You're going like that?" I ask with a smile, and sit up in the bed, taking her in from head to toe. She even has mascara smudged under her eyes because I didn't give her time to take her makeup off before I fucked her brainless last night.

"It's okay if I look homeless," she says with a shrug. "I'm just going through the drive-thru. I'll be back in ten minutes."

"Okay." I grin as she leans over the bed and gives me a sweet kiss. "I'm going to jump into the shower while you're gone."

"Good plan. I'll take one when I get back."

She waves as she walks out of the bedroom, and when I hear the front door shut, I peel the covers off my naked body and pad into the bathroom that we've been sharing the past week. I like seeing our things all scattered together.

Just as I'm leaving the shower and reaching for a towel, my phone rings.

"Hi, sweetheart."

"Trevor," she says, and I can hear the tears in her voice, making every muscle in my body tighten.

"What's wrong?"

"I have a flat tire," she says, her voice full of frustration. "And I look homeless."

My lips twitch, but I know better than to laugh.

"I'll come get you," I reply.

"No," she immediately replies. "I'm a hot mess, Trevor. You don't want to see me like this."

"So you're going to call a stranger to come help you?"

"The stranger doesn't give two shits that I'm braless."

"I'm on my way."

Before she can argue, I end the call and pull on my clothes, rushing out the door to find her. She's pulled into a parking lot just two blocks away from Starbucks.

I park behind her and walk up to the driver's-side window, which she rolls down.

"Hi," I say, and she turns her sad little face to mine. She's not crying, but she has the cutest pout I've ever seen. "Are you okay?"

"No," she says, shaking her head. "I spilled my whole coffee all over me." She holds her cup up for me to see. "I drank the last little drop. And I am capable of changing a tire, but I do *not* want to get out of this car because everyone and their grandmother will be able to see this shit show of an outfit."

"To be fair," I reply, and reach in to tuck a stray piece of hair behind her ear, "you're not a shit show. You're actually quite cute."

"You're biased," she replies, and crosses her arms over her chest, looking thoroughly disgusted with herself.

"I love you," I say with a laugh, and lean through the window to kiss her cheek. "I'm going to fix this. You sit here, and I'll take care of everything."

I just told her I love her.

I shake my head as I walk to the trunk of her car to find a jack and spare tire. This was not exactly how I planned to tell her that I'm in love with her for the first time, but she looked so dejected and sad I just couldn't help it.

I *do* love her, and damn it, I'm going to tell her.

I pull the spare out of her trunk, but when I drop it to the ground, I can see that it's flat as well. It's probably never been used—or serviced, for that matter. So I stow it back in her trunk, shut the door, and walk back to her window.

"I have good news and bad news."

"Okay."

"The good news is, I'm here to help you."

"The bad news?"

"Your spare is flat. I'm going to have to call someone to take care of it."

"Well, shit." She leans her head against the headrest and sighs deeply. "I should have stayed in bed with you."

"But then I wouldn't have the delight of seeing you in this classy outfit," I reply with a grin, earning a glare. "You're adorable when you're pissed off."

"I haven't had any coffee," she says. "And now I have to get out of my car so I can get into yours. Oh no."

"I'm not parked far away," I say reasonably. "I bet no one even notices."

She raises the window, grabs her purse, and makes a mad dash for my rental car, getting in as quickly as she can.

"I haven't moved that fast in years," she says.

"See? No one noticed."

I pull out of the parking lot and back toward Starbucks. We go through the drive-thru and I buy us new coffees, then head home. Riley kisses her coffee cup, making me chuckle.

"I need this."

"And maybe a shot of something to go in it?"

"Nah, this will do."

Riley's quiet as I pull into her driveway and she leads me inside, her flip-flop-covered feet shuffling on the concrete.

I want to scoop her up and kiss the shit out of her.

Once inside, she sets her coffee down and then throws herself into my arms, hugging me tightly.

"I love you too," she whispers, tightening her hold on me. "Thank you for saving me."

"You're welcome."

There's a lump in my chest the size of a grapefruit at her words. I want to ask her to say it again, I want to jump and whoop and freak the fuck out.

Instead, I kiss her temple and breathe her in.

She loves me.

"WE DON'T HAVE to eat here," Riley says the next evening when we arrive at Seduction. We're here at my request. I wanted to come by to say good-bye to the girls.

"Eating Mia's food never sucks," I reply, and kiss Riley's hand. "I'd like to stick around."

She smiles widely and leads me into the bar first, where we find Addie with her husband, Kat, and Cami all at the bar.

"Look who's finally come out of their sex cave," Kat says with a smirk. "Does the sunlight burn?"

"Ha ha," Riley says, and then busts up laughing. "Okay, that's funny."

"I wanted to come in to see you all," I say, and sit in the stool next to Riley.

"You leave tomorrow afternoon?" Addie asks.

"I do." Riley's hand searches for mine. I link our fingers and squeeze. "So I figured we'd better come in so I can eat a Mia meal and say good-bye."

"How are you guys holding up?" Cami asks.

"It's not like he's dying," Riley says, rolling her eyes. She says the words with conviction, but I know she's trying to convince herself at the same time. "Or going off to war. He'll be back soon, and I'll visit him."

"Good," Kat says with a nod. "That's an excellent attitude."

"What are you guys doing here?" Mia asks as she joins us. "If you say you're saying good-bye, I'll throat-punch you."

"You know, I've discovered that Mia is the most violent of all of your friends," I say to Riley, who simply laughs.

"I'm surprised it took you this long to figure that out."

"No." I shake my head. "I saw it early on, but she just keeps fueling my theory."

"What can I get you guys from the kitchen?" Mia asks with a wink.

Riley and I both place an order, and Mia excuses herself to go make us something delicious.

"Are you playing tonight?" Riley asks Jake.

"Yep, I'm going on now," he says with a smile. "Stick around for it."

"Absolutely," she replies enthusiastically. "It's been a while."

We move to a table in the main restaurant, near the small stage that Jake's sitting on, his guitar in hand, and for the next hour, we eat a delicious meal and listen to him. I look around the room and smile with pride. What these women have done here is magnificent. I've been in restaurants all over the world, and this is in my top five favorites.

They've done what they set out to do. It's sexy and fun and romantic.

"Are you okay?" Riley asks, catching my gaze.

"I'm fantastic," I reply, and kiss her hand. "You?"

"I'm good too," she says with a nod and a forced smile. She's been doing that a lot over the past few days as Sunday draws closer. I know she's dreading my departure as much as I am, and she's trying to be brave for both of us.

I also know she'll break down eventually, whether it's in front of me or not. I hate that this is hurting us both. I wish it didn't have to be this way.

But, like her nana told me last week, we don't get to control who we fall in love with.

I thought I'd been in love before. I was married, for fuck sake.

But I've never felt like this before.

Mia brings us a huge molten lava cake with ice cream and two spoons. "Calories don't count when you're sad." She winks and leaves.

"I don't look sad," Riley says to me. "Trust me, I'm working really hard at *not* looking sad."

"You don't," I agree, and kiss her cheek. "You look beautiful, as always. But Mia knows you well, and she knows that you probably *are* sad."

"Well, it's bad form to tell a person that you know that they're sad."

"I didn't follow that," I say with a laugh, and take a bite of the hot cake. "Good God, this is ridiculous."

"It's my favorite," Riley says with a grin. "It's so fucking good."

"I want to strip you naked and fuck you when your mouth is dirty," I reply calmly, and take another bite. Riley's gaze whips to mine and her cheeks flush.

"I wonder what you're really thinking," she says, and

takes a sip of water. "It's a good thing Jake's singing loudly, otherwise every person in here would have heard you."

"I don't care." I hold my spoon up to her mouth, offering her a bite, which she takes. "I'm not shy about how I feel about you, Riley. It's not a secret."

"Now that we're not working together," she says.

"It wasn't a secret before. And we may end up working together again. I have a few ideas to pitch to my boss involving Mia and the whole restaurant."

"You haven't told me this," she says in surprise.

"I don't want to get into details until I know whether it's going to happen," I reply, and lean in to lick a bit of chocolate off the side of her mouth. "Working together doesn't have much bearing on my feelings for you. I'm in love with you."

"Well, pretty much everything you just said made me wet," she says, surprising the shit out of me. "So, there's that."

"There's that," I repeat with a laugh. "I think we'll be leaving after dessert."

"Thank the baby Jesus."

Chapter Fifteen

~Riley~

There is a soccer ball in my stomach.

He's not awake yet, and I don't want him to wake up and see me like this. I thought that I'd had plenty of time to get used to the idea that he was leaving, but I didn't get used to it.

I didn't get used to it at all.

We have exactly four hours left together before he has to go to the airport and turn in his rental car before his flight. Four hours to touch him, smell him, hear his voice, and feel his warmth.

I scoot closer to him carefully, still not ready for him to wake up. If he's asleep, it's not *this day* yet.

I had no idea it was possible to have so much anxiety over a man. And I think it's ridiculously torturous that I finally fell in love with an incredible man just to have him have to leave me.

What the fuck is wrong with me?

He stirs next to me and reaches out, wrapping his arm around my waist. His arms are sexy.

All of him is sexy.

I'm so smitten it's almost sickening.

And I don't want to stop.

"You're overthinking," he whispers in my ear. "Stop that."

"Can't," I reply, hoping he can't hear the tremble in my voice. I'm going to stay strong and not break down until after he leaves. I'll let myself have a good cry then. In the meantime, I need to stay positive and encouraging, and I need to be our biggest cheerleader.

"Do you want breakfast?" His voice isn't as rough as it usually is when he first wakes up, which tells me that he's been awake for a while too.

"I can't eat."

He sighs and buries his face in my neck. "We have to eat, sweetheart."

"I will." I swallow hard and drag my fingertips lightly up and down his arm. "I'll stress-eat later."

"I'm going to get in the shower," he says. "And then I'm going to pack my things really quick so that's out of the way."

I nod, not able to actually form a response that sounds like anything other than *Don't go! Stay here with me! Fuck your life in L.A.*

But that's not fair.

He kisses my cheek and rolls away, walking naked into the bathroom.

His ass really is stellar. Like, there should be songs written about his ass. Maybe I should talk to Jake about it.

I smirk and get up, pulling on clothes as I wander around my bedroom. I gather some of his clothes that he's left in my chair or on the floor.

"Do you want me to wash your dirty clothes real quick?" I call into the bathroom.

"No, it's okay, baby, I'll wash them when I get home."

"Okay."

When I get home.

This fucking sucks.

I hear the shower shut off and walk into the bathroom in time to see him dripping wet before he reaches for the towel and dries off.

"Your body is ridiculous," I murmur, leaning against the doorjamb and watching unabashedly. "Seriously, I don't think that's normal."

He smirks and tosses the towel aside, then strides to me and hugs me close.

"You got dressed," he says.

"I did."

He buries his face in my hair and takes a deep breath. "You didn't have to."

I smile for the first time today and lean back so I can look up at him. "We don't have a lot of time."

"We have enough time," he says. He turns away and

brushes his teeth. I join him, still scrubbing my pearly whites when he leaves the room with all of his toiletries and I can hear him filling his suitcase.

He's rushing about, naked, and when he has everything packed, he returns to me and tucks my hair behind my ear. "There, now I can just focus on you."

"I won't complain about that," I reply with a smile. "Do I sound completely needy if I say that I don't want you to go?"

"No," he says. "And if you do, then I'm needy too because I don't want to go either. But I have to. We knew this was coming."

"I know." I nod and then lean my forehead against his chest. "But I think I've been in denial."

"That's okay too." His hands glide down my arms so he can link our fingers. He walks backward, leading me to the bed.

"I'm already dressed." I wrinkle my nose and yelp when he simply picks me up and tosses me onto the bed.

"Your clothes don't scare me." He makes quick work of removing my clothing, kneeling on the bed, hovering over me. I can't stop touching him, grazing his leg hair with my nails, gliding my hands over his side and belly.

"I like your skin."

"I like *your* skin," he replies, and finally removes the last of the fabric. "You're so beautiful, Riley."

I flush the way I always do when he tells me I'm beautiful, which is often. He kisses my neck as he stretches out next to me, his hands never leaving my body.

"I'm so thankful that I met you," he says. He's moving so

slowly, as if he's memorizing every line of my body. "And I'm incredibly thankful that you decided against the whole friend-zone-only thing."

"Well, this would be awkward, for me at least, if we were just friends." I cup his face in my hands and can't help the tears that spring to my eyes. "I'm going to miss you so much."

"I know." He wipes my tears away and kisses my lips tenderly. "Riley, this isn't good-bye."

"It feels like it." I hold on to his shoulders as he covers me with his body, cradling his pelvis in mine. "It feels like I'm never going to see you again."

"That's absolutely not true," he says. "We're going to see each other, and soon. We'll make it happen."

I nod as another tear falls from my eye. "How can I be so sad and so turned on at the same time?"

A smile dances over his lips as he rears back, rubbing his rock-hard cock against my most sensitive center.

"I'm the same."

He's whispering the way he does in the dark, when it feels like we're telling secrets.

"I love you," I whisper to him. He closes his eyes and sinks inside me, making us both sigh in delight.

"I love you," he replies before kissing my lips, biting the corner of my mouth, and cupping my breast in his palm, brushing his thumb over my hard nipple. "I'm so fucking in love with you."

I smile and then sigh again as he begins to move, guiding

us both to a steady pace of the sweetest, most amazing sex of my life. *This* is what it means to be intimate with someone. *This* is what it means to be in love.

"This is not good-bye," he whispers again as he picks up speed, driving us toward an amazing orgasm. "It's see you soon, my love."

I nod and close my eyes, wanting to feel every inch of him, hear every groan and sigh. I need to memorize this to keep with me while we're apart.

THE DOORBELL RINGS.

"Am I expecting someone?" I ask with a raised brow. We've been snuggled up on the couch, watching a marathon on HGTV and some home improvement show with twin brothers.

"I ordered pizza," Trevor says as he stands and walks to the door. He pays the delivery kid and carries several boxes into the living room, setting them on the coffee table.

"When did you do this?"

"When you were in the bathroom," he says with a grin. "I got extra because I know you'll be stress-eating later."

"Well, there's truth in that theory," I reply with a nod, and frown at the steaming loaded pizza. "There are a million calories in that."

"It's vegetables and bread," he says with a frown, pushing his glasses up his nose. "You'd probably eat all of these things anyway."

"And cheese," I reply with a saccharine-sweet smile.

"Fine, don't eat it." He shrugs as if it makes no difference to him and sits back on the couch with a large slice in his hand, taking enormously huge bites. "Goof."

"What?"

I laugh and watch as he chews and swallows.

"It's good."

"It must be, you're eating it like you've been starving for a year."

"Well, my girlfriend wouldn't let me eat breakfast," he replies. "I think she's trying to starve me."

"I don't remember her denying you food." I take a slice of my own and sit next to him, making sure we're touching from hip to shoulder. "You're awfully dramatic. Besides, you're the one who attacked me and we ended up all naked and tangled until noon."

"That's not how I remember it," he replies, shaking his head in denial. "*You* attacked *me*."

"I did not." I giggle and take a bite of pizza. "I was fully dressed, remember? And you stripped me naked and had your way with me."

"Well, you were the silly one who put her clothes on," he replies. "Don't you know by now that putting clothes on is essentially the same thing as a challenge?"

"No." I wipe my mouth off and laugh. "No, I didn't realize that was the case."

"Well, now you do. And like Mother Teresa says, now that you know better, you can do better."

A giggle erupts from my throat. "Mother Teresa is dead, and she didn't say that."

"How do you know?"

"Because it's one of my favorite quotes. Maya Angelou said it."

"Well, there you go, then." He grins and holds his pizza against my lips, offering me a bite.

"I have my own pizza."

"I'm *sharing*. It's romantic."

He's trying to keep things light during this last hour together, and thank God for it. I don't feel like crying at the drop of a hat anymore.

"Oh, sorry." I take a bite of his slice and moan. "You're right. Yours is better than mine."

"When you make that face, it makes me want to—"

"Let me guess, strip me naked and fuck me?" I bat my eyelashes and he narrows his eyes.

"You've turned into quite the smart-ass."

"I've always been a smart-ass," I reply, waving him off. "You just haven't noticed."

"I've noticed everything," he replies, more serious now. "I'm going to check my calendar when I get back to work and we can talk about a good time for you to come down."

I nod and finish my pizza. "Okay, sounds good."

"Are you going to be okay?" he asks, taking my hand and squeezing it.

"Of course." I smile brilliantly, refusing to let him see me hurting so much inside. "I'm always okay. And you said it yourself, this isn't good-bye."

"Right." He nods and stands, cleaning up our lunch. "I should go. I have to turn in the car."

"I know."

No. No. No. Don't fucking go!

Rather than pick up his bags, he walks to me and wraps me up in his arms, holding on tight and rocking us slowly back and forth.

"Thank you for the past few weeks," he says, his mouth right next to my ear.

"I love you," I reply.

"I know."

And just like that, he's turned a sad moment into a sweet one.

"Okay, Luke Skywalker, you're going to be late."

He stares down at me in horror. "It's Han Solo's line."

"I know." I punch him lightly in the arm. "I was kidding."

He narrows his eyes at me as he reaches for his bags. I walk him out to his car and stand quietly as he loads them in the car. He turns to me and kisses me until my knees are weak, right here in front of my neighbors and God, and then pulls away.

"Be good."

"You be good," I reply. He gets into the car and buckles up, starts the engine, and waves as he backs out and drives away.

That's it.

He's gone.

And I love that he didn't say good-bye.

When he turns and he's out of sight, I turn around and walk back inside. The TV is going, but the house still feels quiet. All of his things are gone. The Xbox is no longer sitting by the TV. His computer isn't on my dining room table.

I wander through the house, and the only thing to remind me he was here is the pizza box in the kitchen.

Just like that, it's as if he's erased from my life.

And it hurts.

It fucking hurts so bad.

So I sit in the chair in my bedroom, where his clothes were lying just a few hours ago, and I let the tears come. I've earned them. I'm going to cry right now, just today and then not again. Because it's not *sad*. We didn't break up, and he's not gone forever, and we will be able to talk all the time. I'll FaceTime him, and I'll be able to see him.

But I can't touch him.

He can't hold me.

And I miss that already. I don't care if it does make me needy and weak and stupid. I don't fucking care in the least.

He's mine and he's gone.

And that's not okay.

I HAVEN'T BOTHERED to turn the lights on in the house. I haven't done much this afternoon except sit on the couch and continue binge-watching the show Trevor and I started this morning. I don't know where the remote is, and I have no energy to look for it.

Not to mention I'm getting really good at this whole home renovation thing. I think I'll have my kitchen redone next. I want one of those farm sinks. They're sexy.

I mean, if a sink can be sexy, those are.

It's dark outside now, the only light is the glow of the TV. Trevor called an hour ago to let me know that he made it home safely and he misses me already.

He's going to call me when he goes to bed tonight.

In the meantime, I'm just going to lie here in the dark and watch TV.

The doorbell rings, and I glare at the door, willing whoever is there to leave. If I had the energy, I'd just yell out, *Leave!*

Instead, I'll just lie here until they get the hint and go away.

"We know you're in there!" Addie's voice yells through the door. Well, shit. The girls are here, probably to make me feel better, but I don't want them to make me feel better.

I want to wallow.

I pull the door open and flip on the porch light, making all four of them squint in the harsh light.

"Fuck, Riley, warn a girl before you do that," Mia says.

"We're here," Cami says proudly.

"You don't say," I reply dryly. "Why are you here?"

"Because we used our Jedi mind tricks and knew that you would need some cheering up," Kat says.

"And we came with provisions," Mia says, holding up wine and a white paper bag full of ice cream.

"You guys—"

"You can't say no," Addie says, and pushes her way past me and into the house, the others following her. "Trevor sent us here to make sure you're not too sad."

"Jesus, it's dark in here," Cami says, searching for the

light switch. "Since when do you become a cave dweller when you're sad?"

"I didn't want to get up and turn on the lights," I reply. "I have pizza. Does anyone want some?"

"Me," Kat says. "I haven't eaten today."

Having resigned myself to having company, I grab the box of leftover pizza and join the girls in my living room. Mia's turned off the TV, and everyone is gathered around the coffee table, some on the couch, some sitting on the floor.

"Why don't you own wineglasses?" Kat asks with a frown as she walks out of the kitchen with regular glasses.

"I only have two, and they're both dirty in the dishwasher."

"You can get more at the dollar store, for God's sake," she says. "You need more than two."

"It hasn't been a problem before today," I remind her, and gratefully accept a glass of cold, sweet wine. "This is my favorite."

"I know," Kat says with a smile.

"How are you?" Cami asks before biting into a slice of pizza.

"Not great," I reply honestly, happy with just the wine. I don't need any more food right now. I ate an entire package of Oreos this afternoon.

"Tell us everything," Addie says. "We haven't seen much of you in the past week."

"Thanks for picking up my slack last week," I say, tears filling my eyes again. "Damn it, I thought I'd already cried all of the tears in the world."

"Oh, honey," Mia says, laying her head on my shoulder and rubbing circles on my back. "I'm so sorry that you're sad."

"I shouldn't be sad." I wipe my nose on the back of my hand in frustration. "I keep telling myself that it's dumb to be so upset. We didn't break up. He's just not *here*."

"You have every right to be upset," Addie says, shaking her head. "This love is new, Ri. It's fresh and exciting. It's the best time in a relationship, and just as you were finding your groove, he had to go. I mean, Jake and I have been together for a couple of years, and I still don't like it when he has to go away for any length of time."

"Seriously," Kat says, nodding, "being in a relationship is exciting, but it's also work. And when you find someone that you just click with, and want to be with all of the time, being away from them is awful."

"It sucks," Mia says. "I know, I'm the one who always says that relationships suck, and I don't need a man, and I *don't*, but I'm not heartless. This isn't easy, and we want you to know that we've got your back. I just wish we could beam you down to L.A. *Star Wars*–style, so you could be with him."

"You just combined *Star Wars* and *Star Trek*," I reply, a smile tickling my lips.

"You know what I mean," she says, rolling her eyes.

"No, no, I don't. Because what you said doesn't make any sense."

The girls laugh and Kat reaches over and takes my hand. "You've come a long way since you met Trevor in my bar."

"I have." I nod, thinking back over the past few weeks

and everything that's happened. "He's really wonderful, you guys. And the sex? Best in my life."

"He's a good man," Cami says with a nod. "Even our guys like him."

"Nana likes him too," I reply. "She says if I don't keep him, she'll steal him from me."

"Just hang in there," Addie says. "Give the distance a chance. Maybe it won't be for long."

"He'd have to move here," I reply helplessly. "And he *can't*. He has an amazing job with a major network. And I can't move from Portland. Nana is here, you guys are here. I own a business. I just don't know how it's going to work."

"With a lot of air miles and faith," Cami says with a smile. "Because he's worth it, Ri."

"Oh yeah. He's so worth it."

Chapter Sixteen

~Trevor~

Call me.

I frown down at my sister's text, surprised that she doesn't just go ahead and call *me*. Not that we talk all that often.

I have a meeting with my boss in ten minutes, so I go ahead and dial her number.

"You're alive," she says, her voice dripping with sarcasm.

"As are you," I reply with a grin. "I've been on location."

"I figured. Are you back in L.A.?"

"Yes, do you need me?"

"It would be nice to see my only brother, yes," she says, and I wince. Colleen is the youngest of us. She's single, and estranged from our parents. I should check in on her more often.

"Let's get together this week," I reply. "Unless you need me before?"

"Well, I do need to talk to you about Stephanie," she says, referencing my ex and making me frown.

"What about her?"

"She's been calling me."

I lean back in my chair and pinch my nose under my glasses.

"And?"

"And, I think she's regretful."

"Of course she is," I mutter, and check the time. "Colleen, I have to get to a meeting with my boss, but I want to discuss this further. Are you available for dinner tonight?"

"Sure. Our usual spot?"

"Sounds great. I'll see you there at six."

"Make it six thirty. I'm coming from across town."

"Okay. See you soon."

We end the call, and I grab a notebook, pen, my cell, and rush over to my boss Chris's office. His assistant smiles and waves as I run by, and Chris's door is standing open, waiting for me.

"Hey," I say as I rush inside. "I'm sorry I'm late."

"You're not," Chris says as he finishes typing something on his computer, shuts it down, and shifts his attention to me. "Did you get in last night?"

"Yesterday afternoon," I reply, and sit across from him. "It's been a busy morning, catching up."

"Understood," he says with a nod. Chris is a great boss.

He's understanding and pretty laid-back, but he expects nothing less than excellence. He's also rather curt in conversation. "I've gone through some of the film from Portland. That was a great call, Trevor. The film is great, and the girls are beautiful."

"Thank you, I think so too," I reply with a nod. "They were all nervous at first, of course, but with time they loosened up, and the filming went quickly."

"Which we all appreciate," he says with a smile. "What do you have coming up?"

We spend the next ten minutes going over possible projects everywhere from Miami to Seattle, and frankly, I'm exhausted just thinking about it.

Which is so unlike me, but now that I've met Riley, the thought of traveling all over the globe for work isn't as enticing as it used to be.

"I'd like to talk with you about another idea," I say just as we're about to wrap up.

"Okay," he says, and leans back in his chair, crossing his ankle over the opposite knee. "What's up?"

"I think the girls *and* Seduction are great enough to do something semipermanent there."

"Add another show to the roster?" he asks with a thoughtful frown.

"Yes," I reply with a nod. "We could start with six episodes to see how well it does, but I love the idea of doing a competition-type show with Mia and a different guest celebrity chef each week."

"It's been done," he says, narrowing his eyes.

"Not like this, and not with Mia. She's brilliant with the camera."

"She has no experience," he counters, and I know I have my work cut out for me with this pitch.

"You said yourself that they're great. The restaurant is beautiful *and* sexy. The kitchen is new and state-of-the-art, and Mia is funny. She looks great in front of the camera."

"She's pretty," he says, rubbing his fingertips over his lips, thinking it over. "Do I sound like a dick when I say that she's not exactly thin?"

"You sound like a network executive," I reply, frustrated. "And so what? We have hosts of all shapes and sizes on our network, and have for years. She's talented, and I think the show would be fun."

"And what if I say yes to pursuing it further?"

"Well, then I'd ask to be relocated to Portland so I could be in charge of the project."

He narrows his eyes on me for a moment.

"What's going on, Trevor? What's happening with you?"

I sigh and close my eyes. I hope I'm not about to commit career suicide.

"I'm in love with Riley."

"Christ, Trevor," he moans, and shakes his head in disappointment. "This is Professionalism 101. Keep your hands off your colleagues."

"The way you keep yours off your assistant?" I ask, and am met with a death glare. "Okay, it's none of my business."

"You're damn right it's none of your business."

"I didn't mean for it to happen."

He rolls his eyes. "Of course you didn't. Who am I supposed to have replace you in your job? The show you just wrapped will still be a show on our network."

"I'm certain there are several qualified people who can take over. Just give it some thought, Chris. I know you can't give me an answer on it right away. Wait until the show is edited and ready to air, then have a look and make up your mind then."

"So, you're not in a hurry to get back up there?" He cocks a brow.

I want to go back right now.

"I would like to go back soon, but we're also not in a huge hurry."

"I'll think about it," he finally concedes, and I sigh in relief that he didn't put the kibosh on it immediately. "And I'll talk it over with my boss as well. It's not a bad idea."

"Thanks, Chris."

"What are you thanking me for? You want to move to Portland."

I laugh and stand to leave, leaning over the desk to shake his hand first. When I get to my office, I glance at my phone and see that I have a text from Riley.

Jesus, I just left her last night, and I miss her so much it hurts.

Just got another message from Angie. Would you please take care of this?

What the fuck? I scowl as I reply.

I'm on it. I'm sorry. I hope you're having a good day.

Jesus, I'm sick of this bullshit. I take a minute to run to the restroom, and when I'm washing my hands, my phone falls in the motherfucking sink.

The sink that has a slow drain, so the phone is submerged.

"Son of a bitch," I mutter, and shake the water off, wipe it off with paper towels, and sigh when I see that it's dead.

Great.

Once back at my desk, I open my Facebook messenger on my computer and bring up the message that Angie sent weeks ago. I never did reply. I'm not afraid to. Conflict doesn't bother me, but I wanted to talk with the other guys first, and frankly, I was putting time with Riley at the top of my priority list.

But I've heard from all of the guys, who agree that she should go.

So she's going to go.

I quickly type out a message to her.

Angie,

I would appreciate it if you would stop communicating with Riley. She and I are very happy together. In light of your recent behavior, the guys and I have decided that it's best if we no longer game together. I wish you well.

Trevor

I hit send and dive back in to work, forgetting about everything except a restaurant in Baltimore that has gotten excellent reviews that I need to go scout out for the show. I'm combing through their website when my assistant calls.

"Um, Trevor, I have a woman named Angie on the phone for you."

Without moving, I shift my eyes to the phone and scowl.

"Are you there, Trevor?"

"Yeah. Sorry. Send her through."

What in the hell is she doing calling me?

My phone rings and I answer on the third ring, taking the time to take a deep breath so I don't tell her to go to hell.

"Angie."

"Hi, Trevor. I must have lost your cell number, so I figured I'd just call your office."

"I never gave you my cell. How do you know where I work?"

"You've mentioned it before," she says with a little giggle. "Are you having a good day?"

"Angie, why are you calling?"

"Because I wanted to discuss your message. Trevor, you can't just kick me out of the gaming group. I've been in it as long as you have."

"But I'm not trying to make trouble in your private life," I remind her, and take my glasses off so I can rub my eyes. "It's already been decided."

"By who?"

"By all of us."

"So, you talked behind my back."

"Angie, you've been sending messages full of lies to my girlfriend. Fuck yes I talked it over with the guys behind your back."

"Riley is not your girlfriend." Her voice is shrill now, and I can't help but wonder just how many issues Angie has. "You and I have something special, Trevor."

"I don't even know you."

"That's a motherfucking lie!" she screams, making me pull the phone away from my ear. "We're in love. Riley needs to back the fuck off."

"I'm telling you this right now. You leave her alone, Angie. Leave both of us alone."

"You're just confused," she says, her voice softer now, but no less full of the crazy. "We haven't talked in a while, and you're confused."

"Angie, get some help. Seriously, this isn't okay."

"Listen to me, Trevor. You belong with *me*, and if you think I'm going to sit back while some cunt tries to steal you away from me—"

"That's enough," I yell, catching her attention. "We're done. I'm telling you again to leave us alone."

She starts to yell again, but I end the call and send a text to Scott.

Angie is officially crazy. We might want to block her from the group.

Without waiting for a response from Scott, I switch over to my text thread with Riley on my desktop.

Hey, babe, I just spoke with Angie. She has some serious problems. Please block her on Facebook so she can't contact you anymore. I'm doing the same on both Facebook and the Xbox. Also, FYI, I dropped my phone in the sink, and now it's acting dead. I'll try the rice trick tonight. In the meantime, I'll have to call from work, or text on my computer.

Both Scott and Riley reply at the same time, agreeing that Angie should be blocked. I promise to call Riley later and set the whole thing aside so I can get through the bulk of my work before I head to dinner with Colleen.

Where I get to talk about my ex-wife, who has managed to avoid starting drama for two years, but seems to think it would be fun to do so now.

Great.

"I BEAT YOU," Colleen says with a smile as I hurry to the table at our favorite restaurant. She stands so she can hug me, then sits across from me.

"I'm sorry, I hope you haven't been waiting long." I take a sip of the water waiting for me and smile over at her.

"I haven't. Just long enough to decide what I want to eat."

"We always get the same thing."

"See? I haven't been here long at all."

I chuckle at her and set my menu aside.

"How are you?" I ask.

"I'm fine. I have a new job."

Colleen switches jobs at least twice a year, much to my dismay.

"Where is it?"

"Disneyland," she replies with a wide grin. "I'm the new Cinderella. Well, one of them anyway."

"You're serious."

I stare at her in surprise. This is the last thing I would have expected because Colleen is *not* a girlie girl. I can't imagine her wearing a big, heavy dress in the Southern California heat.

"I'm totally serious," she says. She's definitely pretty enough to be a princess. "It's fun. Kids love me."

"Of course they do, you're a princess."

"It's nice to hear you finally admit it after all of these years."

I laugh and shake my head. "You've always hated dresses."

"I hate this one too," she says, rolling her pretty blue eyes. "But it's a good job. They have good benefits, and they pay well."

"Those are both good things."

"I can't get medical insurance waitressing," she says reasonably. "And I don't really *like* being a waitress. I'm already used to being on my feet all the time, and now I get to hang out in Disneyland all day. I mean, that doesn't suck."

"No, you're absolutely right. That doesn't suck." I take a deep breath and prepare myself for the next question. "Have you given any thought to going back to school?"

She immediately glares at me. "Stop asking me that."

"No. C, what are you going to do? Be Cinderella forever?"

"Maybe I'll get married and have kids like Lisa," she says, referencing our sister.

"Not that there's anything wrong with that, but you're not even dating. Maybe you should work on a career in case Mr. Wonderful doesn't show up for a while."

"I've been dating," she says, not meeting my eyes now, and before I can grill her further, the waitress stops at our table to take our orders.

After she leaves, Colleen sighs. "I don't want to argue. That's not why I wanted to meet up with you. I've missed you."

"I've missed you too." And it's the truth. She may not be on the fast track to a career in medicine, but she's a hard worker, and takes care of herself very well. She never asks me for help, even though I have a feeling that there are times she could use it, and I have to respect that.

Colleen tilts her head to the side, watching me, as she takes a sip of her soda. "You look different."

"I might have lost some of my tan up in Portland," I reply.

"That's not it." She shakes her head, still watching me. "You look . . . *happy.*"

"I was unhappy before?"

"God, you're a pain in the ass." She throws an ice cube at me. "You seriously look different." She pauses, and then her eyes widen. "Oh my God, did you meet someone?"

"Am I wearing a sign?"

"I'm your sister. I know you. You did. Who is she? What does she look like? Do I know her?"

I grin and pull up a photo of Riley on my phone, then turn it to Colleen. "Her name is Riley, and I met her in Portland."

"Oh, she's pretty," she says, and smiles at me. "I'm *so happy* for you."

"Thanks."

"Wait. She's in Portland?"

"Yes."

"You can't move to Portland." Her eyes fill with tears at the idea, making me soften a bit.

"I'm not packing yet, C."

"No, I mean it. I barely talk to Lisa. I don't see the 'rents at all. You're all I have, Trev. You can't move away."

"Portland isn't far."

"Uh, have you looked at a map? Yeah, it is."

"You never know, you might decide that you want to move up there too."

"I'm *Cinderella*." She rubs her forehead as if she's completely frustrated at me, and I can't help but smile.

"Well, if the whole Cinderella gig doesn't work out, and *if* I move up to Portland, it might be an option."

"You're stressing me out," she mutters, and digs into her fries when our meals are delivered. "And speaking of stressing out, you need to do something about Stephanie."

"I was hoping you'd forget about that."

"Yeah, well, I *can't* forget about her because she's been blowing up my phone like a bill collector."

"Do you have a lot of bill collectors calling you?"

"Jesus, it's a figure of speech. And no, I don't. Focus, Trevor."

"What does she want?"

"She's been getting all sentimental and whining that she thinks she made a mistake with you."

"She gets sentimental every year when it's about to be our anniversary," I remind her. "She usually sends a text, and that's the last I hear from her."

"I know, but why is she calling me and not you?"

"Probably because she knows I won't take her calls. I don't have anything to say to her."

"Well, she's getting more persistent. She called me *four* times last week, and she texts at least once a day to find out if I've talked to you."

"Christ," I whisper, and set my half-eaten burger on my plate, suddenly no longer hungry. "You should block her."

"No, I did that last year and she showed up at my house."

I raise a brow in surprise. "You didn't tell me that."

Before she can answer, my phone rings, shocking me.

"I'm going to take this. I thought my phone died. Hello?"

"Hi," Riley says. Her voice sounds tired.

"Hi, sweetheart. How are you?"

"Fine." She sighs. "I kept busy today. I didn't think I'd be able to get through on your cell, but I thought I'd leave a message."

"It's a miracle that your call came through. Listen, can I call you back? I'm having dinner with Colleen."

She's quiet for a split second, and then, "Who's Colleen?"

"My youngest sister." I wink at Colleen, who looks mildly annoyed that I never told Riley her name. "We're catching up for a bit, and then I'm heading home."

"Okay. I'll be here."

"Thanks. I'll talk to you soon. Love you."

"I love you too." The smile is in her voice now as we both hang up and I turn my attention back to my sister. "Before you complain, I did tell her I had sisters, I just don't think I told her your names."

"You told her you love her." Her eyes are wide and her voice cracks a bit when she says "*love*."

"I do love her."

"I'm seriously *so* happy for you," she says, and reaches over to squeeze my hand. "And for the record, I'm *not* going to tell you that I think you should talk to Steph."

"Good because I'm not going to."

"I know. I told her I'd talk with you. She seems really sad."

"And you're a sweet woman who feels sorry for everyone." She smiles and shrugs one shoulder. "Do I have to remind you that she fucking *cheated* on me, married the dude as soon as the divorce was final, and took me for quite a bit of money in the process?"

"No, you don't have to remind me at all. I don't like her. I didn't like her when you were married to her."

"I know."

"But you should know that she might show up at your house or something."

"She won't, and this will blow over, C. It always does. She's not even a blip on my radar anymore. It's been over for a long time, and I'm finally at a point where I'm moving on. Riley's great. She's smart and funny and so fucking beautiful it almost hurts to look at her."

"Wow," Colleen whispers. "This is the healthiest I've ever seen you. I hope I get to meet Riley, because I'd love to thank her."

"For what?"

"For that sweet look on your face. I don't think I've ever seen it before, even when you were first married. You deserve this, Trev."

"Let's not get too mushy."

"Oh, that's right, you're a guy." She rolls her eyes. "Send her flowers."

"Who?"

"*Riley*. Send her flowers. I'm sure she misses you, and it would make her feel better if you sent her some flowers."

"That's not a bad idea. I'll do it in the morning."

"When are you going to see her again?"

"I don't know," I reply honestly. "We both have demanding jobs, and I took last week as vacation so I could spend some extra time with her, so I'm not sure when we'll make it happen. Hopefully soon."

"Well, if she comes here, let me know and I'll get you guys into Disney. I get family passes."

"That's a cool perk."

"I'm a princess," she says with a smug smile.

"We always knew that."

"Damn right we did." She nods once and steals the check when the waitress sets it on the table.

"I can buy dinner."

"So can I," she says. "Let me treat you."

"Are you sure you don't want anything? You're being awfully nice to me."

"I just missed you," she replies quietly. "Sometimes a girl just needs her brother."

"Okay." I hold my hands up in surrender. "Besides, how many guys can say that a princess bought them dinner?"

"That's the spirit," she says with a laugh. "I'm happy you're home."

"Me too."

Chapter Seventeen

~Riley~

I t's been two weeks," I say to Nana as we sit in our pedicure chairs, getting our feet pampered. Trevor has been gone for two weeks, and I can't say that it's been a good two weeks.

"When was the last time you spoke to him?" Nana asks.

"It's been a couple of days." I lean my head back against the massage chair and take a deep breath. "Honestly, I've heard from him less and less as time goes on. And I understand that we're both busy with work, and his phone is all messed up because he dropped it in the water, but it's hard to not even hear his voice for days on end."

"I can imagine so," Nana replies. "I do know that that boy loves you. I don't believe he's trying to back away from you."

"I don't either, and that's almost harder than if he was. He texts me and tells me he loves me, but he's not making real time for me. I *need* to hear his voice. I need to see him."

"Well, he can't very well just fly up here on your every whim."

"I know, Nana, but he can FaceTime me."

"What does that mean?"

"It's a video call on our iPhones." I smile and pull my phone out of my pocket to show her how it works.

"Well, look at that," Nana says with a smile. "I can start FaceChecking your mama, since she doesn't bother to come see me."

"Face*Time*," I reply with a laugh. "And yes, you should do that. She should go see you more than twice a freaking year."

I don't bother to hide the disappointment and disgust in my voice.

"She's busy too."

"That's an excuse," I reply. "Don't defend her. I run a business and I come see you once a week. And not because I *have* to, but because I love you and I want to see you."

"I know." Nana reaches over to pat my hand. "You're a good girl. I'm sorry that your gentleman caller is making you sad."

"I love it when you call him that," I reply with a soft smile. "It sounds old-fashioned and traditional. Do I have to hand in my feminist card because I like traditional?"

"If you do, I'll hand mine in with you," she says. "There's nothing wrong with wanting a man to be a *man*, and to respect you, Riley, all while you earn an equal wage and have the same rights as a man. I marched in my fair share of women's rights marches through the years for that very reason."

"I know." I nod and hand the tech my nail polish. I always bring my own. The thought of having them use polish that has touched someone else's feet grosses me out. "And I am so proud of you for doing it."

"Having traditional values isn't wrong. And frankly, I'm a bit disappointed in Trevor that he's made you feel insecure."

"I wish I could talk to him in person. Maybe this is all in my head. I do overthink everything. There's a meme going around that says something like '*I have ninety-nine problems, and eighty-six of them are ones I've made up in my head.*'"

"What's a meme?"

"A picture with a quote on it."

"Oh yes, I see those on the Pinterest all the time."

"Exactly. So maybe it's all in my head."

"No." She shakes her head and purses her lips as she watches the tech paint her nails. "I don't think it's in your head. You're a smart girl, and you have good instincts. I'm sure he's not intentionally being distant, but you should tell him that you need him to be more available to you."

"That's going to make me sound needy."

"And what of it?" Nana demands. "Riley, life is short. You already live far away from each other. At the very least, you should be speaking every day. It's not needy to express that you need more from the man you love, and if he says that it is, well, then maybe he's not the man for you."

"He might just be really busy."

"Now who's making excuses for whom?" Nana asks with a smile.

"I know, but it really could be the case." She stares at me without speaking, but I can see her thoughts written all over her face.

Stop making excuses for him and talk to him.

"I'll FaceTime him tonight and talk this over with him. Hopefully he had time to go get a new phone today."

"Good girl," Nana replies with a satisfied nod. "What do you have going on after this?"

"I thought I'd take you to lunch."

"Well, this is a treat. I get to spend all afternoon with you?"

"Of course. And after lunch, we should do some shopping. I need some shoes for Kat's birthday party next weekend. I already have a dress."

"That sounds fun. I could use a new bathing suit for this summer."

I feel my brows climb into my hairline in surprise. "A bathing suit?"

"They're building a new swimming pool in the community, and I want to look good sitting by it this summer."

"You should stay out of the sun, Nana."

"There are umbrellas," she says with a wink. "And we're still a ways from summer, but I might find something fun."

"We will have a look."

"Good. I can cook you dinner if you like."

"Yes, I would love that. Let's make a day of it."

"Let's do that."

I DIDN'T GET to talk to Trevor last night. We texted back and forth, and he said he was tired. He also mentioned that work has been increasingly demanding, and that he misses me very much. I asked him to replace his phone, again, and he promised to put it on his list today.

"If he misses me so much, why won't he fucking call me?"

"What's that?" Kat asks as she walks into the office. She stops short when she sees my face. "Oh God. You're pissed already."

"Men are more work than they're worth," I reply, and toss a folder on my desk. "What's up?"

"Well, maybe I shouldn't talk with you about this now."

"It's as good a time as any," I reply with a sigh.

"No. No, I don't think it is."

"Oh, for fuck sake, Kat, what the hell is it?"

"See? You're very sweary."

I narrow my eyes at her and she clears her throat, then shrugs one shoulder as if to say, *What the hell?*

She pulls her phone out of her pocket and taps the screen until she finds what she's looking for.

"Have you seen this?" She passes the phone to me.

"I didn't know you and Trevor are friends on Facebook."

"We are, because I need to look out for you. Although he's very dull. He *never* posts."

I'm staring at a photo of Trevor and another woman. His arm is slung around her shoulders and they're smiling at the camera.

It doesn't look recent.

"He didn't post this," I murmur. "He's tagged by Angie."

The caption reads *I always love spending time with this guy.*

"What the fuck," I whisper.

"So you haven't seen this."

"I blocked Angie because she kept sending me messages about Trevor, and he asked me to block her so she couldn't cause any more trouble."

"Oh," she says. "So you wouldn't have been able to see this anyway."

I shake my head no.

"I don't think it's recent," Kat continues. "I mean, his hair is a lot shorter in that picture, and he just looks *younger*, you know?"

"Yeah, it doesn't look recent." *But what in the hell is going on?* Without missing a beat, I grab my phone and call Trevor's number, but it goes to voice mail. "Hey, it's me. I need to talk to you. Please call me back as soon as possible."

I hang up and pass Kat's phone back to her.

"I'm sure it's nothing," she says.

"I guess we'll see when I talk to him."

"What are you going to say?"

"I'm going to ask him if he's seen this, and if so, why does it even *exist*? I mean, why won't this chick just go away? She's seriously pissing me off."

"You don't think he's got something going on with her?"

"No." I shake my head impatiently. "I believe him. I think this is *her* trying to make waves again, and I just don't understand why she won't go away. Trevor spoke to her and told her to hit the road."

"Sounds like she's psycho," Kat replies. "And I'm a psychiatrist, so I can say this with some authority. Be careful. People like her are dangerous."

"She doesn't live anywhere near here," I reply. "Maybe it's time for me to take a break from social media for a while."

"Is that even possible for you? With all of the social media stuff you have to do for Seduction?"

"No." I rub my forehead with my fingertips. "You're right, it's not possible. But I can delete the apps from my phone and just post stuff on the computer when I'm here."

"That could work," Kat says with a nod, and turns to walk away. She spins back around, sticking a finger in the air. "Oh! Forgot to tell you. There's someone named Stephanie here to see you."

I frown and glance at my schedule. "I don't have any appointments today."

"She didn't say what she wanted, just asked for you."

"Okay. Thanks. I'll be out in a minute."

Kat nods and shuts the door behind her, leaving me in the office by myself. I wish Trevor would call me back *now*. I wish he would truly talk to me and tell me what's going on with him. I wish his stupid phone would work right.

I trust him.

But I miss him.

And it hurts more than I ever thought it would.

It doesn't look like he can call, so I walk out of the office and to the hostess area. There's a beautiful brunette sitting on the bench, her hair and makeup perfectly seen to. She's in a red sweater and black slacks with red heels.

"Stephanie?" I ask as I approach.

"Yes," she says, and smiles. Her teeth are almost blindingly white against her red lips. "You must be Riley."

"I am. I'm sorry, did we have an appointment?"

"Oh no." She blushes and smiles with apology. "I'm sorry I didn't call ahead, I just thought I'd take my chances that you'd have time to see me today."

"I wish you *had* called. I'm afraid we're not hiring right now."

"Oh, I'm not here for a job." She shakes her head and hooks her expensive designer bag over her shoulder. "This is a personal matter."

"I see."

I don't fucking see at all.

"Come into my office." I motion for her to follow me, and when I get there, I hold the door open for her. "Go ahead and have a seat over there. I'll join you in a moment."

"Thank you."

I rush into the bar and find Kat behind it.

"I'm meeting with this woman in the office. I don't know her, and she says this is personal, not regarding the business."

"I'm coming along."

"Wait." I hold my hand up. "I don't think I have a reason to be afraid, but I wanted someone else to know I'm in there with her."

"I think I should go in with you."

I chew the inside of my cheek for a moment, and then nod. "I guess it doesn't hurt to be careful."

We both walk into the office, clearly surprising Stephanie.

"I'm sorry," she says, clearly not sorry at all. "I was hoping to speak with you privately."

"Kat is my business partner and my best friend. Anything you have to talk about can be said with her here."

She sighs, and then nods. "If that's the way you want it."

I don't reply as I sit in my chair opposite her and cross my hands over my desk. Kat sits at her own desk, facing us.

"My name is Stephanie Cooper."

I blink at her for several seconds. She doesn't elaborate, as if I should recognize her name, but I don't.

"Okay."

She licks her lips and frowns. "You don't recognize my name?"

"No, I don't."

"Riley—" Kat begins, but Stephanie speaks over her.

"I'm Trevor's wife."

And just like that, a cold sweat spreads over my whole body and my heart pounds against the wall of my chest.

"I can see that I've surprised you."

"I'm not sure what you're doing here," I reply, proud of myself for sounding so calm.

"Well, I wanted to come meet you in person. You see, Trevor and I divorced a few years ago."

"I'm aware."

"So he *did* talk about me, then," she says with a happy smile.

"He mentioned an ex-wife, but he didn't ever say your name."

Her smile falters now, and that gives me a sick sense of satisfaction.

"Yes, well, we parted on decent terms."

"Despite you deciding to have an affair," I add. Kat gasps, but neither of us looks over at her. "What do you want, Stephanie?"

"I don't honestly know," she says. "I thought I wanted to come here to tell you to stop seeing him."

"I'm not seeing him," I reply. "He's in L.A. and I'm in Portland."

"Oh, so you're not together."

"We're together. What I'm saying is, it's gone past just seeing each other. We're in a relationship, and we're in love with each other."

"Oh, honey."

"Don't fucking *'oh, honey'* me." I stand and walk to the door, holding it open for her. "If you're warning me off, you came all this way for nothing. I haven't done anything wrong. You're not married to him anymore."

"You're right," she says. "I'm not. I'm actually married to another man, who's also a very good person."

"So, do you just get off on fucking around with people? Why do you care who Trevor is with? You moved on."

"It was a mistake." Her eyes fill with tears, and I give zero fucks. "I made a horrible mistake."

"Yes, you did." I stare down at her, not feeling even one ounce of sympathy. "Women like you just think that the grass is always greener on the other side of the fence. What you don't realize is, if you just took care of your own fucking grass, it would be just as green."

"I'm not much of a gardener," she says with a frown, and I can't help but bust out laughing.

"Like I said, you've wasted your time. Now get your ass out of my restaurant, and don't contact me again."

"I was hoping that I'd be able to talk to you, woman to woman, to make you understand how much I love him. I guess that isn't going to work."

"Um, no, it's not. That's what I meant when I told you to get the hell out of my place."

"Fine." She walks through the door and turns back to me, every ounce the drama queen. "He's going to realize one day that it was a mistake for us to break up, and then he's going to come back to me."

"Whatever." I roll my eyes and slam the door shut, effectively halting anything else she might have said.

"So, the ex-wife is a bit of a drama queen," Kat says as I walk back to my desk and sink down in my chair. "Rough day."

"And it's only ten," I say, and reach over to call the kitchen.

"This is Mia."

"Hey, it's Riley. Would you please have someone bring me a bag of ice? I have a killer headache."

"Coming right up." She hangs up and I cover my eyes with my hand.

"What are you going to do?" Kat asks.

"Well, I've already called him about one crazy girl pining away for him this morning, and he hasn't returned *that* call, so it's a waste of time to try to call again."

Mia walks through the door and passes me a bag of ice.

"You didn't have to bring it yourself."

"I needed a break. My sous chef is gonna drive me to drink."

"Please don't fire another sous chef," I say desperately. "I think this might be the last available one in the Portland metro area."

"I won't fire him," she says, and tucks a stray hair behind her ear. "But I needed out of there for a second. You okay?"

"Aside from dealing with more than one jealous woman where Trevor is concerned, and not having actually talked to said man in the past four days?" I nod sarcastically. "Yeah, I'm peachy."

"Men suck," Mia mutters. "And I get to go back to the kitchen now and deal with one. Let me know if you need anything."

She walks to the door and stops, looking back at me. "Riley?"

"Yeah?"

"You don't deserve that. Any of it. Don't let him get away with it."

"I won't."

She nods and leaves and I rest the ice on my head.

"Oh, that feels good."

"She's right," Kat says.

"I know." I'm glad the ice bag is covering my face because tears fill my eyes. "I love him, Kat. I really do. And despite these crazy bitches who can't seem to get over him, I trust him. But this long-distance garbage is *hard*. I know I'm strong, but I don't know if I'm this strong."

"Talk to him tonight," she says. "And I mean *really* talk. Voice your concerns and see what he says. He might just make you feel better."

"Yeah." I sigh and let the tears fall. "I'll talk to him. If he'll answer my damn calls. He better fucking get a new phone, Kat."

"For sure," she says. "He's pissing *me* off over that one."

It's AFTER EIGHT in the evening when I walk through my door. Work has been *brutal* and I'm exhausted. I might need to talk to the other girls about hiring me an assistant. There's so much on my plate now that I could use the extra help.

Rather than take the time to change my clothes and settle in, I call Trevor right away, immediately using FaceTime.

And he doesn't answer.

"Fucking hell," I mutter, and hit send again. This time he answers after about four rings.

"Hey, babe," he says, and smiles at the phone, and just like that the lead weight in my stomach lifts.

"Hi. I really need to talk to you."

"I know." He looks away from me—toward the TV, I'm assuming, because I can see the lights bounce off his skin. "But tonight isn't great. It's Wednesday, so gaming night."

"Trevor, I *really* need you tonight. I haven't talked to you in days."

"I'm sorry." He pulls the earpiece out of his ear and looks at me. "I know things have been crazy, and that you're tak-ing the brunt of it. I really am sorry. Tonight is kind of a big deal with the guys, and they are counting on me to play with them, but I have *nothing* happening tomorrow evening. We can FaceTime all night if you want."

I want to say no. I want to yell and cry and throw a fit. I hate feeling like his game is more important than me. That his job is more important. That his damn broken phone is more important.

And I have important things to discuss with him, but he's not even paying attention to me anymore. He's already hung that earbud in his ear and is back to playing with the boys.

"Trevor."

"Yeah."

He doesn't look my way.

"Why don't you give me a call after you've grown the fuck up."

I hang up and turn off my phone, then toss it in my handbag and walk away.

Fuck this.

I don't need it. I don't deserve it.

And I won't stand for it.

Turns out I'm not made for the long-distance thing after all.

And fuck me, it feels like my heart is being ripped from my chest.

Chapter Eighteen

~Trevor~

I've spent the morning trying to call Riley and she hasn't picked up the phone, nor will she return my text messages. I'm fucking pissed off.

The last thing she said to me last night was basically grow the fuck up, which I heard all too often from Stephanie, and it never failed to piss me off then either.

My reaction to Riley saying it had the same effect.

She knows that I play on Wednesday nights. That was never a fucking secret, and she said it was fine before. But now that I'm in L.A. it's not okay?

I didn't sleep much last night as I chewed it over in my head, and now this morning she won't pick up, so I'm not in the best mood.

Not to mention, Scott and his wife, Wendy, are due here

at my place any moment because Scott's going to be my Realtor, and if I'm going to move to Portland, I need to sell my place.

I hit send on my phone, and Riley finally picks up.

"Hello."

"I've been trying to call you all morning."

"I know." Her voice doesn't exactly sound inviting. "I've been at work, Trevor. I can't just always pick up when you call."

"I texted too and you didn't respond. All you had to say was that you're busy. I'm frustrated."

She barks out a laugh and I scowl at the phone.

"Oh, *you're* frustrated? Well, I don't know what to tell you. Maybe it's good that you have a taste of your own medicine. Now, I have to go back to work."

She hangs up and I'm left staring at the phone. What the fuck just happened? Before I can call her back and ask her what the hell flew up her ass, Scott and Wendy show up. I slide my phone in my pocket and answer the door.

"I haven't seen you since you've been home," Wendy says, and gives me a hug. "Scott's been telling me all about your love life, so there's no need to fill me in."

"Oh, good," I reply with a smile. Wendy and Scott have been married for the better part of twenty years, and I consider them both good friends.

"So, we're going to sell your house," Scott says, and opens his iPad. "Are you sure about this?"

"I'm sure." I nod and look around my place. "I shared

this with Stephanie, and it's time to sell it. I had to buy her out with the divorce, so I've lost some of the equity, but I'm hoping to come out ahead."

"You should," Scott says. He's a successful Realtor in L.A., usually selling multimillion-dollar homes in West Beverly Hills. "The market is great right now, and your place is in a good location. Take me for a quick tour to refresh my memory, and I'll call in someone to take photos for the website tomorrow."

I lead him through, room by room, while Wendy stays in the living room, working on her phone.

"By the way," Scott says as I lead him into the master, "I tried to call you several times this morning to let you know I was running a little late, and was sent to voice mail every time."

"Well, I was on the phone with Riley."

"For the past three hours?"

I frown. "No. I dropped my damn phone in the water a couple of weeks ago. The rice trick worked, but it's not dependable."

"You might want to go get a new one."

"Yeah, well, I've been kind of tied up with trying to get back to my girl, who is currently pissed at me for said phone, so yeah. Thanks for bringing it up."

"I do what I can," he says, and follows me through the rest of the house.

"So things with Riley aren't great?" Scott asks as we return to the living room. Wendy looks up from her phone, listening.

"I haven't been able to talk to her as much as either of us would like, and honestly, she's pissed at me."

I relay the last few days of conversations, getting frustrated all over again. "I've been busy at work, trying to get things tied up so I can go to Portland. She's acting like I'm blatantly ignoring her."

"Have you told *her* that you're trying to get to Portland?" Scott asks.

"No. I want to surprise her."

"Not a good idea," he says, shaking his head. "Trust me on this one. Just tell her what's going on."

"She knows my phone is screwed, and she knows I've been busy at work."

"That may not be the only problem," Wendy says with a wince. "Have you looked at Facebook lately?"

"No." I scowl as Wendy stands and walks to me, holding out her phone.

"Angie tagged you in this photo."

I read the caption, and stare at the photo we took together the *one* time we met in person, close to ten years ago.

"What the fuck," Scott mutters. "I thought you took care of her."

"I thought so too," I reply with a sigh. "What's her deal?"

"Well, she's clearly crazy," Wendy says, rolling her eyes. "And she has a huge crush on you."

"I don't get it. I barely know her. I mean, I've known her for a long time, but only online. She's nothing at all to me."

"Sometimes you can't explain crazy," Wendy says with a shrug. "Just block her from everything and cut her off at the pass." She continues to scroll through her phone and then gasps. "Holy fuck."

"What's wrong?" Scott and I ask in unison.

"So, this might also have added to Riley's attitude." Wendy bites her lip and looks uncomfortable.

"Show me."

She closes her eyes and turns the phone to us, and my blood begins to fucking boil.

"Steph checked into Seduction." Scott looks from me to Wendy and back again. "That's the name of Riley's place, right."

"Right." I pinch my nose and pace away, then back again. "Stephanie was there *yesterday.* Fucking hell."

"I'm sorry," Wendy says, tears springing to her eyes.

"Why are you sorry?" I ask.

"Well, I still talk to Stephanie. I mean, you don't go from being friends for almost twenty years to *nothing.* And I truly thought she'd be happy for you. She's moved on and seems happy, so I assumed she'd be happy for you too."

"You told her I was seeing Riley."

"I did. I'm sorry, I know it's not my place, I really didn't mean any harm."

"I know," I reply with a sigh. "So, Riley knew all of this last night when she called, and I blew her off."

"Oh. Ouch," Wendy says with a wince. "And if your phone has been shitty—"

"Who knows what I've missed," I finish for her, and curse myself an asshole. "What the fuck am I going to do?"

"Get your ass to Portland and fix it," Scott says. "If you love her, you need to go to her and make it right."

"I can't leave until Saturday," I mutter, already making plans in my head. "I have meetings today and tomorrow, wrapping stuff up. I really want to secure this new show at Seduction so I can present it to all of five of them as a done deal, not just a possibility."

"Can you do that remotely?" Wendy asks. "If I know Steph, I know that she most likely made a huge mess of things yesterday."

"I can't believe she went all the way to Portland." I shake my head in disgust. "What is she trying to accomplish?"

"Well, you can ask her," Scott says, gesturing out of the front window. The woman herself is walking up my sidewalk, a basket of something in her arms.

"Oh, this is gonna be good," Wendy says. "If you think we're leaving, you don't know me very well."

"I'll need the witnesses," I mutter, and pull the door open before she can ring the bell. "What do you want?"

"Hi, sweetheart," she says with a wide smile. "I wanted to come by to say hi and bring you a little present."

"Jesus, you're a piece of work." She walks past me into the house and stops short when she sees Scott and Wendy.

"Oh, hi, guys. Do you mind giving us some privacy?"

"They're staying," I say, my voice hard and unwavering. "You're the one who's leaving."

"I just want to talk." Her voice has a hint of desperation now. "I really miss you, Trev."

"No, you don't."

She sets her basket down and links her hands in front of her, looking down.

"Why are you doing all of this, Steph? It was *you* who cheated and decided that I wasn't enough for you. The divorce was mutual. It's been *years* and you're remarried. What the fuck is your problem?"

"I didn't think you'd move on!" Her chest is heaving at her outburst, and her eyes fill with tears. "I thought you'd just stay single, and the thought of you being with someone else just kills me."

"You're a selfish bitch," Wendy says.

"I never claimed to be anything else," Steph replies with an unapologetic shrug. "If I can't have you, I don't want anyone else to have you either."

"What did you say to Riley yesterday?"

"I told her the truth. That we are meant to be together and she should stand aside."

"Christ," I whisper, and rub my fingers over my mouth. "Listen very carefully because I'm only going to say this one time. I *don't* want you. I never will. We are divorced, and you are gone from my life permanently."

"Trevor," she says, but I hold my hand up, stopping her.

"No. You can't manipulate your way into this. Even if I wasn't in love with Riley, which I am, you wouldn't have a chance. You sealed that the day you decided to let another man stick his dick in you."

"Ew," Wendy says, then seals her lips shut.

"Get the fuck out of here, Steph. If you contact Riley ever again, I'll have a restraining order issued, and I will sue you for harassment."

"You wouldn't dare," she sneers.

"Try me."

"You loved me."

"Past tense. Now you're just some bitch who's hurting my girlfriend. I won't stand for it. If you think I'm bluffing, keep pushing and see what I do."

"Fine." She clears her throat and looks between the three of us. "Wendy will keep me posted on what's going on with you."

"Oh, fuck that," Wendy says. "I'm done with you too. I didn't tell you Trevor's good news so you could dick around with him. I mistakenly thought you were still a decent human being. You can go to hell."

"Fine," Stephanie says again, and walks to the door. She looks back at me dramatically. "You'll regret this."

"Don't fucking threaten me."

She blinks rapidly and leaves, almost jogging to her car, and drives away.

"I'm sorry," Wendy says again, but I shake my head and pull her in for a hug.

"You didn't do anything wrong."

"Okay. Please go find Riley. Make things right."

"Yes, ma'am." I smile as she pulls out of my arms and into Scott's embrace. "You get this house sold. I'll leave my keys with you."

"I'll take care of it."

"I can help too," Wendy says. "I'll have movers come pack you. I'll supervise it all, so you don't have to travel back and forth."

"That would be amazing."

"Don't worry about a thing."

I smile at my friends, and then frown again. "Don't make any calls quite yet. She's still pissed as hell at me, and may not want to stay in a relationship with me."

"She will," Wendy says with confidence. "Once you explain it all, she'll be great."

"Let's hope."

THE MEETINGS TODAY ran late, so it's close to nine when I call Riley. She hasn't answered any of my texts today, but to my surprise, she answers the phone now.

"Hello."

"Hey."

I take a deep breath. "Riley, I need to explain some things to you."

"No, Trevor, you really don't."

"Trust me, I do."

"The thing is, I've been doing a lot of thinking. The past few weeks have been really difficult for me."

"I know, I'm trying—"

"I need to say this before I lose the nerve. I just don't think I can do this, Trevor. I've been so sad and frustrated, and when I've told you that I need you, you're just not there for me."

"But—"

"And I know that you're busy. We both have demanding careers, but I was hopeful that we would make time for each other, and that just isn't happening. Maybe I'm needy. And if that's the case, I'm honestly okay with that, because I *deserve* to be needy, Trevor. You were so attentive when you were in Portland, but that's changed. I love you *so much*, but I am not built for a long-distance relationship."

"Trust me—"

"I *do* trust you," she says, interrupting me again. "That's just it, I totally trust you, but I don't feel like I *have* you, and I can't live with that. So, as much as it hurts, I have to let you go. I wish you nothing but the best in life, Trevor. I want you to be happy, and I genuinely hope you find someone perfect for you."

"Riley—"

"Good-bye, Trevor."

She hangs up the phone and I'm left stunned, staring at the wall. She just fucking *dumped* me.

She thinks it's over.

She thinks that she doesn't have me.

And all of these things are my goddamn fault because I've been too busy living in blinders, chasing the day that I can wrap my L.A. life up and move to Portland.

But in the process I was ignoring the best thing to ever happen to me.

I'm not giving up.

No fucking way.

I immediately dial Chris's number.

"Hello."

"Hi, Chris, I'm sorry to call you so late."

"I just saw you thirty minutes ago," he replies. "It's fine. What's up."

"I'm sorry to do this to you, but I have to leave town tomorrow morning."

"No."

I pause and sigh in frustration.

"Trevor, I've fought for this show that you want in Portland because I think it's a great idea, and I know you're anxious to get back up there, but we have presentations all day tomorrow. I am not going into that boardroom by myself. You will be there, or I'll scrap the project altogether and you can go to Portland jobless."

"Chris, I know you're doing me a solid, and I appreciate it more than I can say. You've been awesome."

"Then you'll do *me* a solid and go to that presentation with me tomorrow. The network doesn't approve new shows on a whim. We're going to need both of us in there tomorrow."

"You're right," I mutter. "Okay, I'll be there."

"Good."

He hangs up, leaving me feeling completely helpless. I need to pull Riley in my arms and feel her. I need to reassure her that I love her more than anything, and that everything is going to be okay.

She's right, being apart has sucked, and I've done the worst thing of all by burying my head in work. It helped mask the loneliness and homesickness for her.

As I look around my place, it occurs to me that I have a lot to do in a very short time. So I call Colleen, who surprisingly sounds like I've just woken her.

"Were you sleeping?"

"Yeah." She yawns. "I spent all day being chased around Disneyland by children. They're fast, Trev. And they like to tug on that heavy-as-fuck dress. One kid *climbed* me today. She climbed me like a motherfucking tree."

"I'm sorry," I reply, my lips twitching. "Are you working tomorrow?"

"No, thank God. I'm not going to move from my bed for about thirty hours."

"Well, about that. Could I maybe talk you into coming to my place?"

"Tomorrow?"

"Now."

"Now." She laughs and I can hear her getting out of bed. "Yeah, I can be there in about thirty."

"Thank you."

"I don't look pretty right now, so don't thank me so soon."

"I don't need you pretty, I just need you."

"Aw, you're such a sweet talker." She snorts. "On my way."

She hangs up and I immediately call my mom.

"What's wrong?" she asks as soon as she picks up.

"Nothing. Well, nothing emergent." I clear my throat, ready to get the *"why don't you ever call me"* speech, but she surprises me.

"What's up, buttercup?"

"Wow, you're not going to yell at me for not calling you more often?"

"Well, that doesn't work, so I'm turning over a new leaf. What's going on, Trevor?"

"Well, I was hoping that I could come over tonight and get grandma's engagement ring."

"Okay, *now* I'm pissed. I didn't even know you were dating anyone, and you want Grandma's engagement ring?"

"I know, and I promise I'll fill you in, but I'm in a hurry."

"This isn't like you."

I sigh and close my eyes. "If the answer is no, just say so so I can make other arrangements."

"Well, don't get all testy," she says. "Of course you can have her ring. She left it for you. I was just relieved you didn't want to give it to that bitch you were married to before."

"Stephanie wanted something more expensive."

"Hmm, should have been a red flag, don't you think?"

"There were lots of red flags, but this woman is different, and I want her to have the ring."

"Then I suppose you should come and get it. And, Trevor?"

"Yeah?"

"I'm happy for you, sweetie."

"Thank you."

Colleen walks through the door just as I hang up with Mom.

"Are you dying? Do I have to take you to urgent care?"

"No, nothing that dramatic."

"Oh, good, because I'm really not going to be able to hurry. My whole body aches."

"I need to walk through the house with you, and show you what I'm going to need for you to do tomorrow while I'm in meetings."

"Good-bye, Netflix," she says with a sigh. "Where are you going now?"

"To Mom's."

She scowls. "I'm not going with you."

"I know. You stay here and I'll be right back."

"Trevor, what's happening?"

"I have to fix things with Riley. Stephanie and Angie screwed things up, and I didn't help."

"Who the fuck is Angie?"

"I'll explain it all as soon as I get back from Mom's."

"Okay." She sinks into my couch and reaches for the remote. "Bring back food. I'm hungry."

"Deal."

Chapter Nineteen

~Riley~

I can do this. I'm going to get through this the same way I have gotten through every other disappointing man in the past: I'm going to pull up my big-girl panties and get on with it.

It's Friday morning. I haven't spoken to Trevor since last night when I told him that it was over. Do I regret it? Well, it depends on the moment. Right now, yes. Because I miss him, and I'm sad.

But then I remember how it felt to have his ex-wife march into my office and stake her claim. I remember how much it hurts that he hasn't communicated with me, and no. No, I don't regret it.

Just as I get into my car to meet Kat and Addie at the gym, my phone pings with a text.

From Trevor.

Good morning. I want to tell you that I love you, Riley. Don't give up on me. I'm coming for you.

"I'm coming for you," I say aloud, and set my phone aside as I put the car in gear and back out of my driveway. "What the hell is that supposed to mean?"

And just like that, I'm reduced to a puddle of tears all over again. I'm so fucking sick of crying. I feel like I'm going to use all of the tissues in the world.

I'm still blubbering like a baby when I pull into the gym parking lot and cut the engine.

"Pull it together, Riley." I turn the rearview mirror so I can see myself, and cringe.

I look like a hot mess.

Which works well because that's exactly how I *feel.*

"Stop it," I tell myself sternly. "He's not worth all of these tears. You're wasting expensive mascara on him, and that's just wrong. I need to invest in waterproof mascara." I wipe my cheeks and under my eyes. "Go work off some aggression with the girls."

Speaking of the girls, Addie yanks my door open. "Are you coming? Our class starts in ten minutes."

"I'm coming."

"I'm not doing yoga," Kat announces. She's got plenty of bounce in her step. Her hair is up in a high ponytail, and she simply glows with happiness.

"Then why are you here?" Addie asks with a frown.

"Because I'm going to run on the treadmill. Running sheds fat faster than yoga."

"Well, until I no longer have my baby boobs," Addie says, gesturing to her tits, "I don't run. They're liable to give me black eyes."

"Sports bras are a beautiful thing," Kat says with a laugh. "But yoga is great too."

"I need to stretch out," I say, and sniff. "I've been curled in the fetal position all night, crying."

"Okay, that's not okay," Addie says. "Not okay at all."

"I know. It was just for one night. I'm done now."

I hope.

"We're going to talk about this after your class," Kat says as she breaks away from us to find a treadmill. Addie and I grab mats and take our places toward the back of the class. I really don't like the thought of sticking my ass in someone's face during downward dog. Although it's a moot point because this room is closed in with glass, so everyone in the damn gym can see in. Basically, I'm still sticking my ass in someone's face.

The instructor arrives, and begins the class, slowly moving us through the various poses. I've always enjoyed yoga. It's a great stress reducer.

And Lord knows I need to reduce some freaking stress.

"How are you really?" Addie whispers beside me.

"Shitty," I reply. "I broke it off with him last night."

"No." Her gaze whips to mine, and the instructor scowls at us.

"Quiet, please."

"Sorry," we both mumble.

"You seriously broke it off?" Addie whispers, and I simply nod.

"He hasn't been talking to me. And there has been some drama, and I'm too old to deal with drama."

"Shh," a woman says in front of us, earning an eye roll from Addie.

"What did he say?" Addie asks, ignoring the glares we're getting from others around us.

"I didn't really give him a chance to reply. But he texted me this morning."

"And?"

"I'll tell you later. Do you see Kat?" We both look through the glass windows. Kat's on a treadmill, running as if her life depends on it. "Why is she running so fast?"

Addie snorts. "Is there a grizzly bear chasing her?"

"Maybe Captain America is waiting at the finish line?"

"Is the treadmill stuck on that speed and she's trapped like a mouse?"

"I think you mean a hamster."

We both giggle, and the instructor sighs in frustration.

"If you could be quiet so the others can enjoy the class, that would be great," she says loudly, making us both giggle.

"We're in trouble," I mutter, and we're quiet for the rest of the class, moving from pose to pose, breathing deeply. It really does feel good to stretch and let my mind empty. I don't even care if people can see my ass. I've been too busy lately trying to guess what's happening with Trevor, and buried under work.

It's a lot to handle all at once.

But by the end of the class, I feel loose and relatively care-free, which is a huge improvement.

"Namaste," the instructor says as we all stand and leave the room. Ironically, Addie is wearing a T-shirt that says NAMASTAY IN BED.

I love this woman.

Kat slows the treadmill down and hops off after her cooldown, panting and sweating as she joins us. "How was your class?"

"It was yoga," Addie replies. "What was chasing after you? You were sprinting."

"The way I figure it, if I run super fast, I can run less often since I'm burning more calories."

"Makes sense," I reply with a nod.

"Okay, Riley was telling me about Trevor texting her this morning, even though she broke up with him last night."

"Wait." Kat stops, holding her hand up. "You *broke up* with him?"

"Yeah. I just . . . I can't do the long-distance thing."

"What did his text say?" Kat asks.

My chin wobbles as I think of his words, so I open the text and show it to them.

"Wow," Addie whispers.

"I don't even know what that means," I say, and stuff my phone in my pocket. "How is he going to come for me? And when? I'm not a freaking mind reader."

"Maybe there's more to it than meets the eye," Kat says.

"I mean, maybe you should give him a chance to explain things."

"No." I shake my head as we walk out to our cars. "I am *not* built for a long-distance relationship. I need him to touch me. I need hugs and kisses and *sex*. Call me shallow, but I do need those things."

"That's not shallow at all," Addie replies. "Hugs and kisses are called affection, and it's a very important piece of any relationship."

"Definitely," Kat says with a nod. "And he hasn't said whether he'd be willing to move here?"

"He hasn't said hardly anything at all." I'm just frustrated again, which is so much better than being sad. "He won't return my calls, even when I tell him that I really need to talk to him. It's like, as soon as he went home, the amazing communication just stopped."

"Yeah, that's not okay," Kat says, and gives me a big hug before she gets into her car. "I'm sorry, honey. Let me know if you need me."

"What are you doing for your birthday?" Addie asks, which is brilliant because while we already know, Kat doesn't *know* that we know.

"I think Mac's just taking me out to dinner," she says with a smile. "We're gonna keep it low-key."

We nod, and wave as she drives away.

"Do you already have a dress?" Addie asks as we both watch Kat drive down the street.

"Yeah, Trevor bought me one." I scowl. "Maybe I should

buy a different one. I don't know if I want to wear something that he bought me."

"Now you're being dramatic," she says. "Wear the dress. Mac said he'll have Kat out of the apartment by three so we can sneak in and get set up, and he'll have her back by eight."

"Sounds good. Cami said she already bought all of the decorations."

"She's so crafty," Addie says with a grin. "It'll be a fun party."

I nod and unlock my car. "I'm going to run home to shower, and then I'm heading into the office for a while."

"Okay. I'm taking today off. I feel like I haven't seen Ella much this week."

"You definitely should go spend some time with her." I hug Addie and smile when she pulls back. "Give her a kiss from me."

"I'll give her lots of kisses from you." She waves as I get into my car and drive away. I feel better. Still not great, but better than I did this morning. I needed the exercise, and I needed the time with my friends. I'm making the right decision. Now the trick will be to stay busy for a while and focus on something besides my broken heart.

CAMI HAS OUTDONE herself. Since Mac and Kat have been gone, the rooftop garden that Kat loves so much has been transformed. Lights hang from anything standing still, and I'm not sure where Cami rented the jukebox from, but it's amazing. Rockabilly music is filling the air, and we're all dressed the part, in fun dresses, our hair in big curls, and bright red lipstick on all our lips.

"You look amazing," I say to Mia, who's hurrying by with a tray of appetizers.

"I'm stuffed so tightly into this dress that I can hardly breathe," she says, but then a smile spreads over her lips. "And I do look amazing."

Everything is ready for Kat, and they should be here any minute. Anyone not working at Seduction tonight is here, along with Kat's parents and Mac's mom and brother, Chase.

Even Mia's parents are here.

It's a full house.

"They're here!" Cami announces, looking down at her phone. We cut off the lights and wait for the door to open, and when it does, the lights are flipped on and we all yell, *"Surprise!"*

"Holy shit," Kat says, her hand on her chest. She looks around, taking in the party decor, and all the people here to celebrate her, and then she launches herself into Mac's embrace, hugging him close. "So much for a low-key birthday."

He laughs and kisses her soundly. "Happy birthday, my love."

Kat wanders through the crowd, hugging her parents first.

"We did it," Cami says, holding her hand up for a high five. "She was surprised."

"Of course she was," Mia says, and sips a glass of champagne. "We're good at keeping secrets."

"We kept this one for a long time," Cami says, then frowns. "What else are you guys keeping from me?"

"Nothing," I say with a laugh. "Don't be so suspicious."

"Thank you, ladies," Mac says as he approaches and offers us each a hug. "You did a beautiful job."

"She deserves a good birthday," Addie says as she pats Ella's back. The baby is in the cutest damn rockabilly dress I've ever seen. She even has a matching headband.

"I'm going to make a toast," Mac says, and wanders off, looking for Kat. "Can I have your attention, please."

We all quiet as we turn our attention to Mac. He has Kat's hand in his, and he's gazing down at her lovingly.

"I just want to thank you all for being here tonight to help me celebrate the birth of the most important person in my life. Kat, you deserve to have the best celebration. You are the most caring, loving, beautiful, funny, and intelligent person I know, and I'm so blessed to call you mine. You make every day better. I'll never be able to repay you for that. Happy birthday, my love."

"Thank you," Kat says, and lets Mac bring her in for a long, close hug.

"I have to go to the restroom," I murmur to Cami, and make a quick exit before anyone else notices. I can't stop the tears falling down my face.

I rush into the bathroom and Cami follows me in, worry written all over her face.

"I heard about Trevor," she says quietly. "Addie filled me in."

"I don't know why I'm crying again." I grab a wad of tissues, then press them to my eyes. "I've cried all of the tears in the world already. I can't turn them off. And I know that

Kat deserves this amazing party, and the wonderful man she has. I'm *so happy* for her, and for you and Addie. I don't begrudge you your happiness in any way."

"I know," Cami says. Her voice is soft and she's rubbing circles on my back soothingly. "But you thought you'd found that too."

"I did." I nod and finally surface from my tissue hell. I finally broke down and bought waterproof mascara, and so far it's worth its weight in gold.

"It's okay to be sad."

"I'm so tired of being sad," I reply, and blow my nose. "Maybe I shouldn't stay. I'm kind of a downer."

"Or you could drink a lot. That usually makes you feel better."

"Honestly, I don't feel like drinking either."

Before she can respond, we both pause as we hear someone shouting.

"Is that Mia?" I ask, and we both hurry out of the bathroom. I stop short when I see Mia yelling at Trevor, whose gaze is on hers. He's not replying, he's just listening as she rails at him in my defense.

Landon is standing behind her, arms folded over his chest, legs shoulder width apart.

"Why does Landon look like the Secret Service?" Cami asks. "Damn alpha man."

"I have to go." Just then, Trevor looks over to where I'm standing, but I don't say a word to him. Instead, I walk over to hug Kat and Mac. "Happy birthday."

"Thanks." Kat smiles. "He looks pretty sad too."

I just shake my head and walk away. Mia calls out to me and hurries to catch me before I make it to the elevator.

"Don't worry," she says. "I'm going to kick his ass. But maybe you should listen to what he has to say."

"Mia—"

"Drive safe."

The doors close and I can't wait to get to my car and speed away. I don't want to speak to him. I don't want to see him.

But when I pull into my driveway and walk up to my house, Trevor pulls in behind me.

"I need to talk to you," he says. Every muscle in his body is tight, his eyes are narrowed. His hair is messy from his fingers.

God, he looks fantastic.

"Trevor, I said everything I needed to say the other night."

"Yeah, well, you wouldn't listen to anything I had to say, so I'm here to say it."

"Fine." I unlock the door and step inside, throw my keys in their bowl, and stomp toward the kitchen, knowing he'll follow me. I turn to look at him from across the room. "Say it."

"You look amazing in that dress."

"I'm quite sure that's not what you were going to say."

And when you say things like that, you make me soft.

"Riley, I don't want to break things off. I'm *so sorry* that Stephanie and Angie caused so much trouble. I had no idea it was happening until after the fact."

"It's not just them," I say, resigned to having this out here and now. "Don't get me wrong, they didn't help at all. But it just felt like the whole situation was full of drama. These women are warning me off my own boyfriend, and when I try to call and talk to you about it, you ignore me."

"I wasn't ignoring you."

"Not returning my calls or texts *is* ignoring me. I need attention, Trevor. I need to see you and talk to you every day. I need to feel like I'm at the top of your priority list. And you obviously can't do that for me."

"I'm such an idiot," he says, pacing the room. "I wasn't ignoring you, I promise. I wasn't getting all of the calls or messages. My phone was fucked up, and I know that's my own damn fault and I should have made it a priority to get a new one, but, Riley, I promise you, I've done nothing but spend the past few weeks doing everything in my power to figure out a way for us to be together full-time."

"You weren't backing away?"

"No, baby." He takes a step toward me, but I step back and he growls in frustration. "Do you know how fucking hard it is to be in the same room with you for the first time in weeks and not have you in my arms?"

"Yes." I cock a brow and wait for him to keep speaking.

"I love you," he says. His chest is heaving, his green eyes on fire. "You're the best thing that's ever come into my life, Riley. Being without you was pure torture, so I put my head down and worked my ass off. If I was working, I couldn't miss you."

"I did that too."

"And I have very good news."

He smiles, and for the first time, hope takes up residence in my heart.

"Go on."

He steps forward, and I don't step away, making him smile wider.

"I came up with a way for me to be in Portland full-time, and for the restaurant to get more exposure and bring in a good chunk of money."

"Okay."

He takes my hand and kisses it, and I can't stand it anymore. I rush into his arms and kiss him, my heart and soul pouring out in love and relief as we cling to each other.

"I missed you so much," he whispers.

"I need you to finish what you were saying."

"Right." He clears his throat and lifts me in his arms. He sits on the couch and cradles me to him. "A new show on the network, featuring Seduction and, more specifically, Mia."

"Is this just an idea, or has it already been approved?"

"You think so much like me," he says, and brushes his fingertips down my face. "That was what I was working so hard on, and why I was unavailable so much. Chris, my boss, and I were coming up with a show proposal and a presentation to give the muckety-mucks who approve these things, and as of yesterday, it's approved."

"What exactly does that mean?"

"It means that if you want me here, I can be here full-time, overseeing the new show. We can be together all the time, Riley. No more long distance, and miscommunication."

"And no more crazy ex-wives or chicks who think they're better for you?"

"No one is better for me, sweetheart. *You* are all I need. Always. What do you say?"

I link my fingers with his and frown as I think it all over. He wasn't avoiding me, he was working hard to be with me, and life was just messy.

That's not necessarily his fault. Sometimes, life is just a pain in the ass.

"Riley, you're killing me here."

Chapter Twenty

~Trevor~

She's not saying anything, and I swear my heart has stopped beating. She's frowning, thinking over everything that I just said, I'm sure.

Finally, she looks into my eyes and smiles.

"Of course I want you here."

Holy shit, I can breathe again.

"That's excellent news because I've already hired a moving company, put my house on the market, and my boss's boss has approved the show."

"Wow, this is fast. This morning I was working on getting over you, and now here you are."

"Getting over me." I stand with her in my arms and walk back to her bedroom. "Maybe I should remind you what you'd be getting over, exactly."

Her lips twitch, but she keeps her face neutral. "I have an excellent memory."

"Really." I set her on her feet and get to work on freeing her from this dress. "This is sexy as fuck on you."

"You've seen it before."

"I feel like I haven't seen you in forever." I stop undressing her and lean my forehead against hers. "I missed you, Riley."

"I missed you too." She cups my face in her hands and tips her chin up, offering herself to me, and it's the sweetest offer anyone has ever given me. I kiss her thoroughly, greedily, as I make quick work of the rest of her clothing, and suddenly she's standing before me naked, aside from her killer red heels.

"Leave those on."

"I like it when you're bossy."

I grin and lean in to kiss her neck. "Lie on the bed."

"Only if you're getting naked too."

"Well, I think this is a naked zone," I reply as she arranges herself on the middle of the bed. She bites her finger, her blue eyes shining as she watches me shed my jeans and T-shirt and then climb onto the bed over her, kissing and licking my way up her amazing body.

"You taste fantastic."

"I almost forgot how good you are with your mouth," she says, and bites her lip. I'm taking my time. There's no hurry, and I want to rediscover every inch of her. I lick the backside of her knee, making her gasp.

"Your knees are so sensitive."

"I had no idea," she mutters, and moans when I nibble the inside of her thigh. "Or maybe it's just your mouth."

"Both." I lick both thighs now, all the way to the crease. "I can smell you."

"I don't know if that's a good thing."

I smirk and kiss her pubis. "It's a very good thing. You're wet."

I glide my fingertip through her wet center and up around her clit, making her moan and circle her hips.

"You're killing me."

"No, baby." I press a kiss to her core and then lick down her lips and up again. "I'm making you feel alive."

Her hips buck when I suck on her clit, and her hands grasp on to my hair, holding me firmly in place.

As if wild horses could pull me off her right now.

"I want you," she says.

"And you'll have me."

"Now."

I stop and look up at her, her chest heaving with each breath. Her nipples are hard pebbles, begging for my mouth.

And they'll have it.

"We're going to take our time, sweetheart."

"I've waited too long for this to take our time."

I pull myself up and over her, thread my fingers in her hair, and kiss her deeply.

"I can taste myself."

"Do you like that?"

She nods.

"I don't want to rush this, Ri. I feel like I was without you forever, and then I thought I wouldn't ever be here again. I just want to enjoy every second of this."

"Trust me, I'm enjoying it."

I pinch her nipple and she yelps, then laughs. "Okay, okay."

I press a kiss her to lips, her cheek and neck, and then I camp out at a nipple for a while, kissing and biting. Tugging. Her hips and legs are shifting in pure pleasure.

"You're beautiful."

Her navel piercing is screaming out for me, so I kiss my way down and tug it with my teeth and then place wet kisses all around it.

"I think you should get your piercing back." My thumb presses on her clit, waking her up again. "If you want it, that is."

"You don't have a problem making me come," she says, and shakes her head when I replace my thumb with my mouth and suck her. "I don't need it."

"Good."

And now I can't wait any longer. I go to fucking town on her, fucking her with my fingers and kissing her until she falls apart, crying out and shivering, then coming back to earth.

I need her.

Now.

Unable to wait, I cover her once again and brace her legs on my shoulders as I slowly slide inside her.

"Holy fuck," she groans.

I couldn't agree more.

I thrust slowly, shifting my angle and watching her face. She's flushed now, and so fucking responsive I have to look away or I'll come myself.

But then she clenches around my cock, her muscles tightening in another orgasm, and I can't control it. I come with her, groaning as we both ride it out.

When I can move again, I fall to the side of her and wrap my arm around her waist.

"You're good at that." She drags her nails lightly up and down my arm.

"I was just reminding you."

"Thanks."

I kiss her cheek and sigh, finally content.

"I love you, Riley."

"I love you too."

Her voice wavers, catching my attention. She has tears in her gorgeous eyes, and it tears me apart.

"Hey, don't cry, baby."

"I'm sure it's just a physical reaction to so many orgasms right in a row."

She's so fucking adorable.

"I'm sure that's it."

"And I'm relieved," she admits with a whisper. "I didn't want to lose you."

"You were never in danger of losing me."

She nods and wipes her tears away.

"You need to know, right now, that I don't do well with

drama. It's one of the reasons that I had so many issues with dating when you met me. I don't play games, Trevor."

"I know."

"And suddenly your past was in my face."

"I'm so sorry. I promise you that they have both been dealt with."

"I trust you. I never *stopped* trusting you. I didn't think for a second that you were cheating on me with either of them."

"Thank you for that."

"You wouldn't do that. You've had it done *to* you, and I know you wouldn't put me through it."

"Never."

"So I mostly thought they were pathetic. And they both wanted to stir the pot."

"Which, I guess, they succeeded in doing," I reply. "But no more."

"My biggest problem was not hearing from you. I'm too needy for that."

"Okay, we're going to squash this right now," I reply, feeling my blood begin to boil. "You are *not* needy. Stop saying that. You need attention from me, and I'm your partner, Riley. You should have all of the attention that you need and more. I don't ever want you to feel guilty for asking for what you need from me."

"It's a knee-jerk reaction," she admits. "And you're right, it's not *needy*, especially because we're in a committed relationship."

"Exactly. Don't speak about yourself that way anymore. You're putting yourself down, and that's not right."

"You're good for me," she says. "I hope you've got a new phone."

"I need to take care of that soon." I kiss her chin. "I was in too big of a hurry to get up here, so I didn't have time to go in and swap it out."

She laughs and wraps her arms around me, hugging me close.

"Thank you for coming for me."

"Always, love. Always."

I'M SO DAMN nervous," I say to Cami one week later at the restaurant. I've arranged for Mia to make Riley's favorite food, a special pizza that apparently only Mia knows the recipe to, wine, and mini carrot cakes for dessert.

Not to mention the diamond ring currently burning a hole in my pocket.

"You're going to be great," Cami says as she puts the final touches on our table. Kat took Riley out to get her nails and feet done, along with a shopping trip.

All on my credit card.

And everyone we love is here, but hidden. Kat's surprise party gave me an idea for how I wanted to propose to Riley.

Nana and Colleen are chatting in the bar, both looking at Colleen's phone and laughing. Even my mom is here, but Colleen has yet to speak to her.

I wish those two would figure their shit out, but at least they're both here for me today. My other sister, Lisa, couldn't make it, but Colleen promised to take a video and send it to her.

"They're on their way," Cami says with a grin. "I'm going to lead Riley in here to you, and after she says *yes*, we'll all come rushing in to congratulate you and then we'll have dinner."

"*If* she says yes."

"She will." Cami winks and scurries around to make everyone hide, in the kitchen or behind the bar.

If seems like an hour goes by before Riley walks into the restaurant, a frown on her pretty face.

"Why aren't we open?" she asks.

"Because I asked the others to close tonight," I reply, and reach my hand out for hers. "Did you have fun today?"

"I got pampered and went shopping. Few days are better than this one."

God, I hope that's the truth.

Kat sneaks into the bar, and I'm left with Riley, about six dozen flowers, candles, and a ring.

Now it's time to make some promises.

"I love you."

She smiles widely and pushes up on her tiptoes to kiss me.

"I love you too."

I take a deep breath and decide that the speech I'd prepared is dumb. The right thing to do is to speak from the heart.

"Riley, I need to tell you a story."

"Okay," she whispers.

"It might be autobiographical."

Her lips twitch. "I like those kinds of stories."

I nod and lick my lips. "I wasn't looking to fall in love

when I met you. I was excited about the opportunity to feature your business on television, but beyond that, I had no expectations. In fact, the week after we wrapped filming, I was supposed to fly to Miami to scout out another place.

"But then I met you, and I *knew* that you were going to be an important part of my life. I'm so glad that every other man before me fucked up so colossally. I'm so happy that they were all idiots, because they gave me the opportunity to show you how a woman should be treated.

"They gave me the opportunity to fall in love with you, and for you to love me in return. Riley, I'm not a young man. I'm not over the hill quite yet, but I'm experienced. I failed at this once before, and in that experience, I learned some very important lessons, the most important of which is trust. Mine and yours. Trust is a choice, Riley, and that's something that we've always had for each other.

"And in that same vein, *love* is a choice. Every day, even when you're pissed at each other. It's a decision, that even though I may be disappointed or frustrated, or you may be ready to smack me on the back of the head, we will continue to choose love. The trust and the love go hand in hand for me, and that's where I failed before. I'd chosen someone whom I certainly didn't trust, and we chose not to love.

"I won't do that again. With you, I've learned that there can't be one without the other. Just like there is no me without *you*."

Tears are falling down Riley's cheeks as I sink to one knee and pull the ring out of my pocket, holding it up. Riley's hands cover her face, but she continues to watch and listen.

"So, I'm asking you today, with all the love and trust in my heart, to marry me. Continue being my partner, my love, my life."

"Trevor," she whispers.

"Will you marry me, Riley?"

She nods and sinks to her own knees, cupping my face in her palm.

"Of course I'll marry you."

I slip the ring on her finger and pull her to me, kissing her like crazy. Suddenly we're surrounded by everyone. They're applauding, whistling, and the girls are crying.

"Everyone's here?"

"I thought you'd like to celebrate with the people you love the most."

We stand together, and I wrap my arm around her shoulders, not willing to let her go quite yet.

"She said yes!"

"We heard," Nana says as she hugs Riley. "Congratulations, sweet girl."

"That was a great speech," Mia says. "It's worthy of my pizza."

"Wait, you made pizza?" Riley asks, her eyes as wide as saucers.

"That and carrot cake," Mia says, smiling with satisfaction. "This man pays attention. You should keep him."

"Oh, I plan on it." Riley lifts her lips to mine. "I'm absolutely keeping you. I love you."

"I know."

Epilogue

One day later . . .

~Riley~

$\mathcal{S}$hould we start inviting the guys to our brunches?" Addie asks the following day. We're at our usual brunch place, just the five of us, drinking mimosas and eating a lot of food.

Like, a *lot* of food.

It's our Sunday tradition.

"You just got engaged last night," Mia says with a frown. "I can't believe you're here."

"Yeah, why aren't you in the sex cave?" Kat asks.

"I was in the sex cave all evening," I reply, and shift in

my seat, not just a little sore today. "Taking a break isn't a bad thing."

"She can go back to the sex cave later," Addie reminds us all, and chooses an orange muffin from a platter. "I'm so happy for you, honey."

"Thanks. I can't stop staring at my ring." It's a beautiful halo ring, with a round diamond in the center. "Trevor said it was his grandmother's."

"That's sweet," Cami says with a smile. "It's gorgeous."

"I know." I'm beaming, and I don't care. I just got engaged, and I'm the happiest girl in the world. "Oh, and I have some news for you guys."

"Please don't tell us you're already pregnant. I mean, let's take some baby steps," Kat says with a frown, making me laugh.

"No. No babies for a while. I have work news. Trevor has arranged for us to have a permanent show on Best Bites TV."

"Wait," Addie says, holding up a hand. "We're going to have a camera crew around permanently?"

"We're starting with six shows to see how it goes, and then they'll renew from there. And, it's not necessarily going to center around the entire restaurant. They'll be focusing on one aspect."

"No," Mia says, immediately shaking her head.

"The kitchen," I confirm. "Here's the thing, Mia; they loved you. You're a natural in front of the camera, and you're beautiful. It's a great combination."

"What kind of stuff do they want her to do?" Kat asks.

"They want her to go head-to-head in a cooking competition with a celebrity chef. They haven't decided if it's going to be the same chef each week, or if they'll switch it up each week."

"Why me?" Mia asks. "You guys, I admit the show we already filmed wasn't bad, but I don't really want cameras in my face all the time."

"Trevor is looking into using a studio so you don't have to have cameras in the kitchen. It'll be a set made to look like your kitchen."

"Wow, the network is throwing a lot of money at this," Addie says.

"They are. Mia, it's a great opportunity for you. You'll be compensated well."

"Do they know who the celebrity guest is?" she asks.

"They already booked Camden Sawyer," I reply, and try to hide my wince behind my champagne glass.

"No way," Mia says, shaking her head adamantly.

"Come on, Mia, Camden was a long time ago," Addie says. "It's been close to ten years since you've even *seen* him."

"Absolutely not."

"Mia—"

"I said no," she says, and stands. "I will *not* do a TV show with my ex-husband."

She marches out of the restaurant, and the four of us are left staring at each other in shock.

"Did she just say he was her *husband*?" Cami asks.

"She did," Addie replies.

"Well, shit," Kat says. "This is going to be interesting."

Beauty of Us Menu

Mia's Special Pizza

Hand tossed dough with Basil marinara, Applewood
smoked bacon pieces, Soppressata salami, Fennel sausage,
caramelized onion, Fresh mozzarella and Balsamic glaze

Abacela Dolcetto, Umpqua Valley, Southern Oregon, 2012

Siduri Pinot Noir, Willamette Valley, Oregon, 2015

Mini Carrot Cakes

Sineann Riesling Auslese, Willamette Valley, Oregon, 2013

Mia's Special Pizza

Dough:
14 oz. Warm Water (100° - 115°F)
0.65 oz. White Sugar
0.365 oz. Dry Yeast
22.4 oz. Bread Flour
1.8 oz. Extra Virgin Olive Oil
0.215 oz. Salt

1. Combine water, sugar and yeast. Let sit for 5–8 minutes while yeast begins working an aromatic foam begins to form on top.
2. To a mixer fitted with a dough hook, add the flour, oil and salt. Start mixer on low speed and add the water/sugar/yeast mixture and mix until combined.
3. Turn the mixer to medium high speed and mix dough until fully developed, 8–10 minutes.
4. Place into oiled bowl and cover with plastic wrap. Let sit for 45 minutes, the dough will double in size. While dough is fermenting, assemble toppings and make sauce.

Pizza Sauce:

2 cloves of garlic, minced
1 T olive oil
1 can tomato paste
2 t. dry Italian Seasoning
1 ½ cups water or chicken stock
1 T. fresh basil chopped or more if desired
Salt and pepper to taste

1. In saucepan over medium heat, sauté garlic with olive oil until fragrant, about 30 seconds, not too long or garlic will burn and become bitter.
2. Add Italian seasoning and tomato paste. Cook for 2 minutes to "toast" the tomato and add a little flavor.
3. Add water or chicken stock and simmer for 5 minutes. The sauce needs to thicken and cook down a little, excess water will make a runny pizza.
4. Add basil and salt and pepper to taste. Set aside until crust is ready to be topped.

Toppings:

Applewood Smoked Bacon, cut into pieces, and cooked until crisp
Soppressata Salami, thinly sliced
Fennel Sausage, cooked and sliced
Caramelized onions
Fresh mozzarella, grated or sliced
Balsamic glaze

To finish pizza:

1. Punch dough down and begin forming into pizza crust. This can be done by rolling out on a floured surface or manipulating by hand and tossing in air.
2. Place dough on lightly spray perforated round pan. Adjust crust on pan so the dough comes to the edges and almost over the top (there will be some shrinkage during baking). Prick raw crust lightly with fork so bubbles do not form during baking.
3. Place pan into 450°F oven for 8 minutes.
4. After removing crust from oven, add sauce and spread evenly over the top.
5. Add all toppings, except the balsamic glaze. Add the fresh mozzarella that has been grated or sliced last.
6. Place topped pizza back in oven and bake for an additional 6–8 minutes until all toppings are hot, cheese is melty and bubbling.
7. Remove from oven and drizzle balsamic glaze over the top. Cut and enjoy!

Carrot Cake

2 cups sugar
1 ½ cups vegetable oil
4 eggs
1 t. vanilla extract
4 cups finely shredded carrots
2 cups flour
2 t. baking powder
2 t. baking soda
1 t. salt
1 T ground cinnamon
¾ cup finely chopped pecans or walnuts (preference)
¾ cup shredded sweetened coconut

1. Preheat oven to 350°F. Prepare ½ sheet pan by spraying with pan release spray and inserting parchment paper on bottom.
2. To make cake beat vegetable oil and sugar on high speed, until smooth and lights, about 4 minutes.
3. With mixer on low speed, add vanilla and eggs one at a time, scraping down the sides of the bowl and mixing well after each addition.
4. Add the shredded carrots and mix on low until combined.

5. Add the flour, baking powder, baking soda, salt and cinnamon and mix until smooth.
6. Add the pecans and coconut and mix.
7. Spread onto prepared baking sheet and bake for 15–20 minutes until completely baked through and toothpick inserted in center comes out clean.
8. Set aside to cool completely.

Cream Cheese Frosting

1 pound cream cheese
½ pound unsalted butter
2 pounds powdered sugar
1 T. vanilla extract

1. Combine all ingredients in mixer and mix until fluffy and combined.
2. Fill piping bag fitted with star attachment and set aside.

To assemble cakes:

1. Use 2 ½" - 3" ring molds and cut cake so you have 12 pieces of cake. (If you can get more cuts out of your sheet, you can make more cakes).
2. Separate the cake rounds in to two piles, 6 on each side. On one round, pipe a rosette of frosting, top with the second round and then another rosette of frosting. Decorate the top of the cakes with sprinkles, candied carrots or edible flowers.
3. Hold extra cakes, covered, in the refrigerator for 2–3 days.

Jake's song for Addie, "If I Had Never Met You,"
specially written and recorded for *Listen to Me*, is
available for purchase from music retailers!

Kristenproby.com/listentomesong

Coming next from Kristen Proby, the final sizzling romance in her *New York Times* bestselling Fusion series,

SAVOR YOU

Cooking isn't what Mia Palazzo does, it's who she is. Food is her passion . . . her pride . . . her true love. She's built a stellar menu full of delicious and sexy meals for her restaurant, Seduction. Now, after being open for only a few short years, Mia's restaurant is being featured on Best Bites TV. To say Seduction is a wild success is an understatement. All the blood, sweat, tears, and endless hours of work Mia has put into the restaurant has finally paid off.

Then Camden Sawyer, the biggest mistake of her life, walks into her kitchen . . .

Camden's celebrity chef status is world-renowned. He's the best there is, and the kitchen is where he's most at home. He can't resist the invitation to Portland for a showdown against Mia for a new television show. Mia was in his life years ago, and just like before, he's met his match in the beautiful Italian spitfire. The way she commands the kitchen is mesmerizing, and her recipes are clever and delicious. He's never had qualms about competition, and this is no different. He can't wait to go head to head with Mia. But can he convince her the chemistry they share in the kitchen would be just as great in the bedroom as well?

As Mia and Camden face off, neither realizes how high the stakes are as their reputations are put on the line and their hearts are put to the ultimate test.

Pre-order now!

BOOKS BY KRISTEN PROBY

LISTEN TO ME
A Fusion Novel
Book One

Seduction is quickly becoming the hottest new restaurant in Portland, and Addison Wade is proud to claim her share of the credit. But when former rock star Jake Keller swaggers through the doors to apply for the weekend gig, she knows she's in trouble. He's all bad boy . . . exactly her type and exactly what she doesn't need.

CLOSE TO YOU
A Fusion Novel
Book Two

Since the day she met Landon Palazzo, Camilla LaRue, part owner of the wildly popular restaurant Seduction, has been head-over-heels in love. And when Landon joined the Navy right after high school, Cami thought her heart would never recover. But it did, and all these years later, she's managed to not only survive, but thrive. But now, Landon is back and he looks better than ever.

BLUSH FOR ME
A Fusion Novel; Book Three

When Kat, the fearless, no-nonsense bar manager of Seduction, and Mac, a successful but stubborn business owner, find themselves unable to play nice or even keep their hands off each other, it'll take some fine wine and even hotter chemistry for them to admit they just might be falling in love.

THE BEAUTY OF US
A Fusion Novel; Book Four

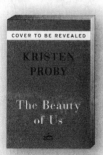

Riley Gibson is over the moon at the prospect of having her restaurant, Seduction, on the Best Bites TV network. This could be the big break she's been waiting for. But the idea of having an in-house show on a regular basis is a whole other matter. Riley knows it's an opportunity she can't afford to pass on. And when she meets Trevor Cooper, the show's executive producer, she's stunned by their intense chemistry.